THE CENTRAL SCHOOL OF SPEECH AND DRAMA

UNIVERSITY OF LONDON

Please return or renew this item by the last date shown.

The Library, Central School of Speech and Drama,
Embassy Theatre, Eton Avenue, London, NW3 3HY
http://heritage.cssd.ac.uk
library@cssd.ac.uk
Direct line: 0207 559 3942

CONSTRAINTS ON PULAAR PHONOLOGY

Mamadou Ousmane Niang

University Press of America, Inc.
Lanham • New York • London

Copyright © 1997 by
University Press of America,® Inc.
4720 Boston Way
Lanham, Maryland 20706

3 Henrietta Street
London, WC2E 8LU England

Library of Congress Cataloging-in-Publication Data

Niang, Mamadou Ousmane.
Constraints on Pulaar phonology / Mamadou Ousmane Niang.
p. cm.
Includes bibliographical references and index.
l. Pular dialect--Phonology. 2. Pular dialect--Accents and
accentuation. I. Title.
PL8184.Z9P8565 1997   496'.3227--dc21   96-45200 CIP

ISBN 0-7618-0611-3 (cloth: alk. ppr.)

♾™ The paper used in this publication meets the minimum
requirements of American National Standard for information
Sciences—Permanence of Paper for Printed Library Materials,
ANSI Z39.48—1984

DEDICATED TO

MY FAMILY AND FRIENDS

WITH LOVE AND GRATITUDE

CONTENTS

CHAPTER 2: SYLLABLE STRUCTURE CONSTRAINTS

CHAPTER 3: CONSTRAINTS ON GEMINATION

CHAPTER 4: METRICAL STRUCTURE CONSTRAINTS

ABBREVIATIONS

sing.	singular
plur.	Plural
di.	diminutive
bilab.	bilabial
lden.	labiodental
alv.	alveolar
pal.	palatal
vel.	velar
glot.	glottal

ACKNOWLEDGMENTS

I am greatly indebted to a number of people who, in one form or another, contributed toward the making of this study. I am greatly indebted to Professor Charles Kisseberth, Professor Jennifer Cole, Professor Eyamba Bokamba, Professor Charles Stewart at the University of Illinois at Urbana-Champaign, Professor Michael Kenstowicz at the Massachusetts Institute of Technology for their advice, guidance, critique, and support. For data collection, consultation and manuscript formatting, I would like to acknowledge the financial support of Dean James During and the Department of English Language and Literature at the University of Missouri-Kansas City. Finally, my deepest gratitude goes to my parents, my brothers and sister, my wife Michelle and my friends. I am grateful to them for their love, sacrifices, patience and continued support.

INTRODUCTION

This book deals with various phonological issues. It focuses primarily on the metrical structure of Pulaar, a dialect of Fula spoken mainly in Mauritania, Senegal, The Gambia, Mali and Guinea. It provides a comprehensive analysis of the metrical system of Pulaar at the word and sentence levels. Two compelling reasons led to the particular focus on the metrical structure of Pulaar. First, previous and numerous attempts to analyze the metrical structure of Pulaar are inadequate. Second, the analysis of Pulaar metrical Structure shows the need to go beyond the binary admitted syllable weight distinctions, an argument supported by various processes that obtain in the language. The analyses adopted show that Pulaar not only breaks this binary distinction but also makes a four way weight distinction in contrast to other views according to which only a two way weight distinction prevails in languages (Hayes, 1989). The analysis of the metrical system of Pulaar shows that stress assignment is sensitive to the "sonority" hierarchy of the syllables in the word. Four sonority levels (CV < CVC < CVV < CVVC) are distinguished for the syllables. In addition to providing a satisfactory account of Pulaar metrical structure, phonological and morphological processes, the analyses adopted in this study show the inadequacy of previous analyses by Taylor (1953) McIntosh (1984), Prunet and Tellier (1984), Paradis (1992) and Bakovic (1995). In addition to focusing on the metrical structure of Pulaar, this study deals with Pulaar syllable structure and gemination. It is argued in this study that constraints on syllable structure are responsible for many phonological processes that obtain in the language.

The first chapter deals with Halle and Vergnaud's (1989) model. The use of this model is motivated by several considerations. The model is well designed. Even though this framework assumes a binary distinction, it can still be adapted to account for the metrical structure of Pulaar. The parameters and conditions suggested in this model are pertinent to the adopted analysis and the facts of the language under investigation. The second chapter focuses on the syllable structure. Various reasons obviate the inclusion of this chapter into this study. First, the processes addressed in the gemination and metrical structure chapters are attributed to constraints on syllable structure, thus the need to provide an analysis of the syllable structure of the language. Second, the analysis of the metrical structure rests on the structure of the syllables involved in the string. The concept of sonority, initially confined to segments (Selkirk, 1982a; Goldsmith, 1990) is extended to syllables. The chapter on gemination provides a comprehensive analysis of the constraints on gemination processes. This chapter is motivated by two important considerations. First, previous analyses of gemination processes in Pulaar (Paradis, 1992; Bakovic 1995) did not provide a satisfactory account of gemination in Pulaar. Second, word initial gemination in Pulaar has not been accounted for in previous studies. The chapter on metrical structure constraints assesses previous accounts and provides a comprehensive analysis of Pulaar metrical structure. In addition, the adopted analysis, based on syllable "sonority" hierarchy, clearly shows the inadequacy of other views according to which only a two-way-weight distinction prevails in languages.

CHAPTER 1

THEORETICAL FRAMEWORK

THEORETICAL MODEL

Introduction

Constraints in phonology have been addressed in various studies (Prince & Smolensky, 1993; Hanson, 1995; Hayes, 1995; Hanson and Kiparsky, 1996). Language constraints impose various restrictions concerning how elements in a particular language can be arranged. Some constraints are specific to particular languages. Certain languages may show similarities in the way they impose restrictions and differences in, not only the types of restrictions that are permitted but also in how potential "violations" of these restrictions are "handled", "repaired" so that violations do not become actualized. Restrictions can be imposed at various levels. This book is an analysis of various constraints in Pulaar. Various processes are analyzed that show a correlation between the constraints and the types of processes that obtain in the language. The constraints in question are analyzed in relation to Pulaar syllable structure, gemination of consonants, and metrical structure.

Stress has been treated as a relational entity where a stressed syllable is more prominent than an unstressed one. This relational aspect has been dealt with using binary branching trees in which S (Strong) dominates the prominent syllable and W (Weak) the weak syllable. This pairing of S & W sequences leads to foot formation. Another important aspect in stress analysis assumes that phonological systems are hierarchical in nature. The relational aspect alluded to above can apply at various levels of the hierarchy. This attempt of characterizing stress is not devoid of problems in that it does not always account for certain prominence distinctions. In an attempt to deal with this deficiency, Liebermann and Prince (1977) suggested the use of the segmental feature which indicates the presence or absence of stress in their metrical theory of stress.

Prince (1983) suggested another simpler approach to capturing relative prominence of syllables. His approach consisted of using what is known as metrical grids using asterisks assigned to syllables and feet. The metrical feet can be right or left headed, bounded or unbounded. Another concept used in this framework is that of extrametricality which refers to syllables which are insensitive when stress rules are being assigned.

1.1) Halle and Vergnaud's Model

The framework adopted for the analysis of Pulaar metrical structure is that of Halle and Vergnaud (1987), a version of Prince's (1983) approach. The adoption of this particular framework is motivated by two considerations. First, this framework is a major improvement over other existing approaches. Second, the apparatus used in this framework can be adapted to account for Pulaar metrical structure.

In this framework, stress is represented on a "separate autosegmental plane" using metrical constituent structure whereby phoneme sequences are represented on one line and stressed phonemes are marked on another line. On line 0, all stress bearing units are marked with asterisks. Another line which represents the stress line is constructed. The construction of the stress line is subject to language particular rules since languages have different ways of building constituents. The element in the constituent that is more marked is referred to as the head of the constituent. The other elements represent the domain of the constituent. Only one element is marked in the constituent.

The following illustrates the suggested representation.

```
tal ku  ru              "charm"
(*   *)<*>      0
 *              1
```

1.1.1 Parameters

Halle and Vergnaud set different parameters that guide the construction of constituents.

Headedness

The headedness parameter indicates whether a constituent is head terminal. That is, whether "the constituent is adjacent to one of the constituent boundaries". A constituent is head terminal if its head is adjacent to one of the constituent boundaries. A constituent is not head terminal if its head is not adjacent to one of the constituent boundaries. A constituent is either [+HT] (+head terminal) or [-HT](-head terminal).

Boundedness

Boundedness, another parameter used in this framework, shows whether a constituent is bounded or not. That is, whether " ... the head of the constituent is separated from its constituent boundaries by no more than one intervening element".

A constituent is bounded if its head is separated from its constituent boundaries by no more than one intervening element. A constituent is unbounded if its head is separated from its constituent boundaries by more than one intervening element. [+BND] indicates that a constituent is bounded; [-BND] indicates that a constituent is unbounded. This parameter is illustrated in (1) and (2).

   1 [-BND]
```
        *
    (*    *    *) <*>
    Nur  tu  Nur  tu
```

   2 [+BND]
```
        *
    (*    *) <*>
    tal  ku  ru
```

The rules that construct metrical constituent boundaries also indicate whether boundary construction starts from right to left or from left to right. The parameter headedness determines whether constituents are left-headed or right headed.

Left Headed Constituents
A constituent is left headed if its head is located at the left end of the constituent as in (3).

3

```
         *
(*      *) <*>
tal    ku  ru
```

Right Headed Constituents
A constituent is right headed if its head is located at the right end of the constituent as in (4).

4

```
          *
(*      *) <*>
gay naa  ko
```

The above parameters are important for determining metrical constituents.
Halle and Vergnaud supplement the above parameters with conditions that determine the application of metrical rules.

1.1.2 Conditions

The Recoverability Condition
Essentially, the Recoverability Condition indicates a reciprocal relationship between boundary and head location in a particular constituent.
In addition to the Recoverability Condition, other conditions help regulate the construction of constituents.

The Exhaustivity Condition
The Exhaustivity Condition regulates the construction of constituent boundaries by specifying that no position can exist that is not part of a constituent.

The Maximality Condition
Essentially, this condition indicates that the construction of constituents is subject to maximality so long as the structure requirements are satisfied.

The Faithfulness Condition

According to the Faithfulness Condition, "rules must respect the asterisks that mark the intrinsic heads."

The Domino Condition

The Domino Condition focuses essentially on the reconstruction of structures altered by the application of rules such as epenthesis.

The Directionality Condition

The Directionality Condition guides rules concerning the construction of bounded constituents. According to the Directionality Condition, bounded constituents are built from right to left or from left to right.

Extrametricality

Another important concept in Halle and Vergnaud's framework is that of extrametricality. An element is marked extrametrical when it is invisible to the rules of constituent construction. Extrametrical elements are found either at the end or at the beginning of strings.

Following the discussion of the parameters and principles (conditions) set in this framework, an analysis of how constituent structures are constructed in this framework is provided. Essentially, constituent construction involves two steps. The first step concerns the construction or the identification of boundaries. The second step involves the location of heads which is subject to the Recoverability Condition.

The analysis that is presented in this study stresses the viability of the parameters and conditions/constraints set within the specified framework. The analysis of the Pulaar metrical system rests basically on the sonority hierarchy among the syllables. Sonority hierarchy is a concept that has been used to refer to segments using a sonority scale system whereby segments are arranged from less sonorous segments to more sonorous ones (Selkirk, 1982a; Goldsmith 1990). This analysis uses or rather extends this concept of sonority hierarchy to syllables. In essence, "syllable sonority" is defined as pitch elevation and loudness. As suggested in the literature (Taylor, 1953), syllables with long vowels have a higher pitch elevation than syllables without long vowels. In other words, given the working definition of syllable sonority in this study, syllables with long vowels are more sonorous than syllables without long vowels.

The analysis of constraints on syllable structure and gemination uses a theory of the skeletal tier.

1.2 The Theory of the Skeletal Tier

The theory of the skeletal tier can be divided into two models. The CV model and the X-theory (or X-slot model). The CV model and its variant the X-theory model are viewed as segmental theories of the prosodic tier because of the correspondence that is established between the number of prosodic elements and the segments in an utterance.

1.2.1 The CV Model

The CV tier model was originally proposed by McCarthy (1979) who used a multi-tiered approach in studies of classical Arabic to show that prosodic templates are necessary for the representation of sequences of CV elements. McCarthy's model was later extended by Clements and Keyser (1983) who required that the theory of the syllable subsume at least the following
a) state universal principles governing syllable structure
b) state syllable structure typology thus defining the range within which syllable structure may vary from language to language
c) state language specific rules governing syllable structure
   Clements and Keyser's model makes a distinction between a phoneme and the position occupied by that particular phoneme in phonological structures. An important aspect of Clements and Keyser's model is the presence of a third tier (CV-tier) mediating between the syllable tier and the segmental tier.
   In this theory, syllable trees consist of three-tiered representations. The syllable tier consists of strings of the root node &. The CV-tier (skeletal tier) which consists of CV elements. The segmental tier which consists of consonants and vowel segment feature matrices.
   These representations are illustrated in the following structure.

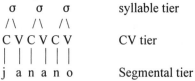

```
σ    σ    σ        syllable tier
/\   /\   /\
C V C V C V        CV tier
| | | | | |
j  a n a n o       Segmental tier
```

The linking is done by means of association lines which are subject to the well-formedness conditions. A segment dominated by a C-element of the CV-tier is nonsyllabic. A segment dominated by a V-element is syllabic. Clements and Keyser advocate the Onset First Principle (Kahn 1976; Clements and Keyser 1983) to determine which syllable node are C-elements assigned in cases where they could be assigned with either the preceding or the following vowel. Syllabification and resyllabification rules apply cyclically following the application of rules such as glide formation, vowel epenthesis and vowel deletion.

1.2.2 The X-Slot Model

The X-slot model used in this study is a variant of the CV theory model. Proponents of the X-slot model such as Levin (1985) and Kay and Lowenstamm (1986) proposed replacing C and V symbols by a sequence of slots (empty positions) represented as X's. This proposal is mainly motivated by the fact that a skeletal position can associate with either a vowel or a consonant. In this theory, the syllable is viewed as consisting of an obligatory constituent and two optional constituents. The obligatory constituent (the rhyme) must dominate at least one V-slot on the skeletal tier. The rhyme is further divided into a nucleus dominating a V-slot and a Coda which dominates the consonant(s) following the vowel of the nucleus. The consonant(s) preceding the vowel of the nucleus is/are the onset. Both onset and coda constituents are optional while the nucleus is obligatory. In the X-slot model, syllables can have the following representations.

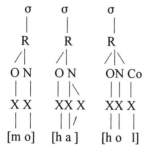

σ = syllable node. O = onset. R = rhyme. N = nucleus. Co = coda.

In the X-slot model, syllabification rules are defined over the skeletal X-slots and phonological weight is determined with regards to the presence or absence of two skeletal positions. In addition, long vowels and long consonants are distinguished from short ones by the association of two successive skeletal positions.

LANGUAGE BACKGROUND

Introduction
The dialect whose sound system is being investigated in this study is called Pulaar. Pulaar is a dialect of Fula which is generally classified as a member of the West Atlantic branch of the Niger-Congo (Greenberg, 1966).

1.3 OVERVIEW
Several terms (Ful, Fulɓe, Fula, Fulfulde, Fulani, Fellati, Fulakunda, Fuutanke, Fulanka, Fulaniyiin, Peul) are used to refer to this language. Some of these denominations clearly refer to the people, not the language itself, as it can be observed form the plurality used in some of these terms. For instance, the term Fulaniyiin in Arabic is obviously used to designate several Fulani people. Some of these terms have a regional denomination in that they refer to the speakers of Fula in a certain area. For instance, the term Futanke is used to designate the Fula of the Fuuta region on the North and South of the Senegal river.

I retain the term Fula as a cover term for the language, a choice motivated by considerations two of which are addressed here. First, despite the use of these various terms, Fula and Fulfulde tend to be used as cover terms. Unlike Fula, Fulfulde can be used to refer to a certain variety of the language. For instance, the term Fulfulde can designate the variety spoken in Mali or a variety spoken in some areas in Nigeria. Unlike Fulfulde, Fula is never (to my knowledge) used specifically to refer to a certain variety. Second, the radical Ful-/Fula is found in most of the terms used to refer to the language or to the people in general.

Fula is argued to be a member of the West Atlantic branch of the Niger Congo Language Family even though this classification is still subject to controversy as discussed in the section dealing with the controversy over the classification of Fula.

1.4 THE DIALECTS

Introduction

A systematic study of the dialects of Fula is yet to be undertaken. Several dialects have been identified just like various terms are used to refer to the language and its speakers.

Previous Classifications

Arnott's Classification

Arnott (1970) identified six dialects.
1) Fuuta Tooro (Senegal)
2) Fuuta Jaloo (Guinea)
3) Maasina (Mali)
4) Sokoto and Western Niger
5) "Central" Northern Nigeria and Eastern Niger.
6) Aadamaawa

This classification excludes the dialects of Burkina Faso, Portuguese Guinea, Mauritania and Benin. The exclusion of these varieties from the above classification is motivated by the fact that the excluded varieties are similar to the dialects listed above.

Westermann's Classification

Westermann and Bryan (1970), following Cremer (1923) also distinguish different dialects of Fula.
1) Futa Senegalais (dialect Pulaar)
2) Futa Djallon (dialect Fula)
3) Macina, Haute Volta, and the Niger bend.
4) Northern Nigeria, with main centers Kano and Katsina.
5) Nigeria: Adamawa Province and adjacent territory.
6) Nigeria: Bauchi Province and parts of the Plateau Province.
7) Bagirmi (dialect Foulɓere)

Dialect Comparison

In what follows, the Pulaar dialect is compared to various other dialects to illustrate the differences that exist between Pulaar and the other Fula dialects. The following comparison is essentially based on Labouret (1952).

The Maasina Dialects

Even though the Massina Dialects are very similar to those of the Pulaar dialects, differences between these two sets of dialects can be noted.

Borrowings

Unlike the Pulaar Dialects in which one notes various borrowings from languages such as Wolof and Sereer, the Maasina Dialects rarely exhibit borrowings from Wolof and Sereer. The borrowings in the Maasina dialects are generally from Mande languages.

Phonological differences.

Various phonological differences exist between the Maasina and Pulaar dialects.

-Vowel/consonant alternation

In the Pulaar dialect, many words can begin with a vowel. In contrast to the Pulaar dialect, in other dialects, many of these words will begin with the glide /w/ specially with verbs as illustrated in the following.

Pulaar	Maasina	
O ari	O wari	S/he came

This phonological difference is an important one because it can result in a difference in meaning. For instance, `O wari' (he came) in the Maasina dialect would mean (he killed) in the Pulaar dialect.

-Initial Consonant Alternation

Pulaar	Maasina
nj	ng
njeenaari	ngeenaari
g	b
gumɗo	bumɗo
k	y
ko	yo

-Medial Consonant Alternation

Pulaar	Maasina
w	b
tawi	tabi
nawi	nabi

-Final Consonant Alternation

Pulaar	Maasina
t	y
potat mi	potay mi
njalat mi	njalay mi

The Fuuta Jalon Dialects
Borrowings
The Fuuta Jalon Dialects are characterized by various types of borrowings from different origins. The vocabulary of the Eastern Dialects is marked by borrowings from Berber, Arabic and Mande languages.

Phonological Differences
-Vowel Lowering e ---> a

Pulaar	Fuuta Jalon
yehi	yahi

-Consonant Alternation
  w/y alternation

Pulaar	Fuuta Jalon
dewel	deyun
m/n	
Pulaar	Fuuta Jallon
lomtaade	lontaade
lamdaade	landaade

The Fula Eastern Dialects
These dialects are spoken in Niger, Nigeria and Cameroon.
Borrowings
Most of the borrowings in these dialects come form neighbouring languages such as Haousa and Zerma.

Phonological Differences
-Consonant Alternation
Implosive/glottal stop alternation

Pulaar	Eastern Dialects
ɗ	ʔ
joɗɗin	joʔʔin
meɗen	meʔen

w/ʔ alternation

golloowo	gollooʔo
baañoowo	baañooʔo

The Volta Dialects
The Volta dialects are used in the areas of Bandiagara, Ouahigouya, Dori, Bobo Dioulasso, Samo, Gaoua, Ouagadougou, Kaya, and Gourma.

Borrowings
The Volta dialects are marked by various borrowings from Soninke, Sonrhai, Mande, Berber and Arabic.

Phonological Differences
-Consonant alternation

Pulaar	Volta dialects
h	f
huɗo	fuɗo
y	s
leydi	lesdi
d	t
ardaade	artaade
g	j
gite	jite
m	n
comcol	concol
r	l
rewɓe	lewɓe
mb	m
mboddi	moddi
nd	n
nde	ne
tiinde	tiine

-Medial implosive drop and its replacement by a glottal stop

feƳƳude   fe?ude

The available classifications present a number of shortcomings. First, not all Fula dialects are subsumed under these general classifications even though these unclassified dialects are different from the dialects in these broad classifications. Second, very similar dialects are classified under different groups.

Conclusion

The discussion in the preceding section compared classifications of the various Fula dialects. The characteristics of every dialect were given and these dialects were contrasted with the Pulaar dialect. A more detailed and comprehensive study of the Fula dialects is yet to be undertaken.

1.5 CLASSIFICATION

Introduction

The purpose of this section is to further investigate the controversy concerning the classification of Fulani. In order to investigate the controversy in question, I analyze the various positions that have been adopted regarding this controversy and discuss arguments espoused by the proponents of the particular position. Then a description of the characteristics of the languages in a particular group is provided to determine whether these characteristics are consistent with the facts of Pulaar, the dialect of Fulani that is used to shed light into the controversy. In addition to discussing Meinhof's position the paper will provide an analysis of the arguments and criteria used by Westermann and Greenberg to classify Fulani either outside of the West Sudanic or in the West Atlantic sub-group of the Niger-Congo respectively.

The controversy over the position of Fulani has been a long one. Friedrich Wilhelm Muller, in his attempt to classify African languages, proposed a Nuba-Fula group; one of the six groups that he had suggested. Muller used nonlinguistic criteria such as skin color, hair type and mode of subsistence in establishing his classification. Meinhof, in his Die Sprachen Der Hamiten published in 1912 suggested that Fulani belongs to the Hamitic group. The studies of Faidherbe (1875), Klingenheben (1914-15), Delafosse, Homburger (1939) and Greenberg (1949) indicated close relationship between Fulani and the West Atlantic languages.

The controversy which represents the major focus of this section involves Meinhof, Westermann and Greenberg's positions.

Meinhof's Classification

According to Meinhof (1912), Fulani belongs to the Hamitic group. This classification is heavily influenced by theories according to which Fulani people are of Caucasoid origin. He attempted a comparative study of Fula, Hausa, Somali and Masai to show that these languages are Hamitic.

Meinhof's Arguments
-Verbal Derivations
   Fulani, like other Hamitic languages, shows a system of verb derivation. The causative suffix {-I} which is present in Hamitic languages is argued to be present in Fulani. In Fulani, however, the causative suffix is not {-I} as suggested by Meinhof. The causative suffix takes the {-IN} form as illustrated in the following forms.
   waal
   wall-in
   laam
   lamm-in

-Initial Consonant Alternation
   Another argument used by Meinhof to show the Fulani Affiliation to Hamitic languages rests on the existence of initial consonant alternations in the noun with specific reference to the personals and the non personals. In the personals, the alternation operates in the following manner: a stop in the singular is realized into a fricative in the plural. For the non personals, a fricative in the singular is realized as a stop in the plural. This alternation, as indicated by Greenberg, is contrary to the facts of Fulani in which the shape of the initial consonant depends on the suffix-class not on personal or non personal meanings.

-Use of Lexical Evidence
   Meinhof made use of lexical evidence to show the affiliation of Fulani to the Hamitic group. Here again, Greenberg shows that Meinhof's comparisons are unlikely to yield any affiliation between Fulani and the Hamitic languages used. He shows that the examples used "tato, tati" in Fulani are closer to the Niger-Congo forms "tat, tato" than Hamitic forms

such as "saddeh, sakua" used by Meinhof.

Having discussed some of the arguments proposed by Meinhof and refuted by Greenberg and data from Fulani, attention is then turned to some major characteristics of the Hamitic languages to determine whether these characteristics are valid for Fulani. The motivation for using the general characteristics of Hamitic languages is that if Fulani is indeed a Hamitic language, it is expected to show features and characteristics that are typical of Hamitic languages. As the scope of this section is rather limited, only some of these general characteristics are discussed.

Hamitic Languages

The name Hamitic is generally used to refer to a group of languages spoken by people called Berbers, Kabyles and Moors. This group (Hamitic) consists of inflected languages. The characteristics of the Hamitic languages analyzed here (numberm gender, case, conjugation, voice, tense, word order) are mainly based on the ones described by Meinhof (1912).

-Number, Gender and Case

Number, gender and case in nouns are expressed by means of suffixes.

-Conjugation, Voice and Tense

Conjugation, voice, and tense in verbs are formed by the use of both prefixes and suffixes.

-Derivative Forms

This group of languages is characterized by the existence of several derivative forms, verb conjugations.

-Case

Case is expressed by means of inflections.

-Gender

There exists a distinction between masculine and feminine gender in all Hamitic languages. The most usual sign of feminine gender is /t/.

-Word Order

The general word order in these languages is VSO

Relevance of Hamitic Characteristics

The listed characteristics of the Hamitic languages are analyzed to determine their consistency with the facts of Pulaar.

-Gender Distinctions

In Pulaar there is no grammatical gender. Unlike Hamitic languages which express gender by the use of suffixes, gender in Fulani is expressed by the use of a distinct word or by the addition of the words for female or male as shown in the following examples.

  -use of a different word

  nagge (nde) vs ngaari (ndi)

  -addition of words for female or male

Given the word "mawniraado" (older sibling), the distinction between an older brother and an older sister is signalled by the addition of "gorko" or "debbo". Thus:

  mawniraado debbo "older brother"

  mawniraado gorko "older sister"

-Conjugations, Voices, Tenses

Conjugation, voice and tense in Pulaar are expressed only by means of suffixation. Hamitic languages use both prefixes and suffixes. As far as voice is concerned, Fulani differs from Hamitic languages in that Fulani has three voices: active, reflexive and passive.

-Use of Derivative Forms

Even though both Hamitic languages and Fulani use derivative forms, the forms of these derivative forms are different.

-Case

Contrary to what obtains in Hamitic languages, case in Fulani is not signalled by means of suffixes. In Fulani, case is expressed by means of prepositions and by position in the sentence. The genitive, however, operates in the same fashion in both Fulani and Hamitic languages in that the genitive follows its governing noun.

-Articles

All Hamitic languages make a distinction between masculine and feminine gender by the use of suffixes. This gender distinction by suffixing does not exist in Pulaar. In Somali for instance, the definite article is "ki" for the masculine and "ti" for the feminine. In Fulani, however, the definite article for both feminine and masculine is "o" for the human class.

-Word Order
Unlike Hamitic languages whose word order is VSO, the word order in Fulani is SVO. The VSO word order can also be obtained in Fulani but it is not the dominant one:
-Fulani SVO
Mi yii Muusa
S V O
-Fulani VSO
Njii mi Muusa
V S O

The above discussion has shown that the major features of the Hamitic languages are not characteristic of Fulani which exhibits differences with respect to the aspects that have been described. Given all these differences, one is inclined to refute the classification of Fulani among the Hamitic language group.

Meinhof's position is supported by scholars such as A. Werner (1925) who asserts that "...the Fulbe or Fulani of West Africa... are Hamitic by race and language."

However, Werner's support of Meinhof's position is not without reservation as he says "if, again, we compare Fulani with Berber, Galla or Somali, we shall find some great important differences."

Having analyzed Meinhof's position and given evidence of the invalidity of his position, I shall now turn to Westermann's position.

Westermann's Classification

Westermann (1911) deals with the Sudanian language family. In his study he excludes Fulani from the West Sudanic group even though he carried out a comparison of the Fulani noun classes with those of the West Sudanese languages and found that the resemblances between Fulani and West Sudanese languages are very obvious. General characteristics of the Sudanian languages which are compared to the facts of Fulani. Here again, the underlying assumption is that if the general characteristics of the West Sudanic fit the facts of Pulaar/ Fulani, the conclusion will be that Westermann is not justified in excluding Fulani from the West Sudanic group. If the facts of Pulaar do not fit the general characteristics of the Sudanian languages, Westermann's position for the exclusion of Fulani from West Sudanic will be justified.

The following table displays the West Sudanic family as described by Westermann (1927).

WEST SUDANIC
I) KWA
II) BENUE-CROSS
III) TOGO-REMNANT
IV) GUR (=VOLTAIC) (including SONGHAI)
V) WEST ATLANTIC (excluding FULA)

Sudanian Languages

The Sudanian languages have been observed by Werner (1925) to share the following characteristics.

-Monosyllabic Basis
The great number of the words and especially the verbs are monosyllabic

-Absence of Inflexion
Even though grammatical relations exist in these languages, they are not marked by inflexions.

-Gender
Gender does not exist in these languages. Even though sex distinction is made in these languages, this distinction is not expressed by means of change in the shape of the word.

-Number
The indication of plurality is not clear-cut. Plurality is sometimes expressed by repeating a word or by the joint use of a word expressing number or quantity.

-Case Features
There is no difference of form between the subject and object of the verb. This difference is signalled mainly by position. In the genitive case, the genitive precedes its governing noun.

-Tenses
The verb does not undergo changes in conjugation, either in the singular or plural.

-Absence of Prepositions
The role of prepositions is supplied by verbs and nouns.

Relevance to Pulaar

-Monosyllabic Basis
Sudanian languages are monosyllabic. That is, the majority of words, verbs in particular, are monosyllabic. This feature of the Sudanian languages seems to hold as far as Pulaar verbs are concerned. Verbs in their root form are generally monosyllabic. However, as far as nouns are concerned, this characteristic does not seem to hold in Pulaar in that nouns in general tend to be polysyllabic.

-Absence of Inflection
Like Sudanian languages, Pulaar is not an inflectional language. There is no grammatical gender even though other devices are used to indicate gender distinctions.

-Plurality
As far as number is concerned, there are marked differences between Sudanian languages and Pulaar. Unlike Sudanian languages in which plurality is expressed either by word repetition or by the joint use of another word, plurality in Pulaar is expressed by initial consonant alternation of the word and the change of the class. These two operations occur simultaneously. Plurality can also be expressed by the addition of a plural suffix as illustrated in the following example.

        sing.   galle (o)
        plur.   galleeji (ɗi)

Both ways of marking plurality apply to certain nouns. That is, the initial consonant alternation and the addition of a plural suffix must occur for plurality to be expressed in certain nouns as illustrated in the following example.

        sing.   horeeru
        plur.   koreeji

-Case Features

Like Sudanian languages, in Pulaar, there exists no difference of form between the subject and the object of the verb. Like the Sudanian languages, the genitive precedes its governing noun in Pulaar.

-Tenses

The tense system is highly developed in Pulaar. Unlike Sudanian languages, the verb in Pulaar can undergo changes in conjugation. For instance, the singular and plural forms are marked by the alternation of the initial consonant as illustrated in the following.

Mi yahii toon   I went there
Min njahii toon   We went there

Another difference between Sudanian languages and Pulaar is that tense differences in the former languages are marked by the use of auxiliary verbs while in the latter, tenses are marked by suffixes.

-Absence of Prepositions

Sudanian languages are characterized by the absence of prepositions whose function is fulfilled by verbs and nouns. In contrast to these languages, Pulaar uses prepositions of different kinds.

The discussion of Westermann's position concerning the classification of Fulani has shown that certain characteristics of Sudanic languages are similar to those of Pulaar. Some facts of Pulaar are different from certain characteristics of Sudanic languages. In view of this, one cannot easily support or refute Westermann's position. However, Werner, 1925 rejects the classification of Fulani as a Sudanic language when he says "Fulani is not a language of the Sudanian type, as is quite evident when we compare its structure with that of Tshi or Ibo."

The next component of this section deals with Greenberg's position about the classification of Fulani.

Greenberg's Classification

Greenberg (1966) includes Fulani within the West Atlantic sub group. Greenberg's position centers essentially around establishing a genetic relationship between Fulani, Serer and Wolof. This motivation aims at establishing a genetic relationship between Serer-Sin and Wolof whose membership to the West Atlantic group has been clearly established. Therefore, establishing a genetic relationship between Fulani and Serer and Wolof will lead to the inclusion of Fulani into the West Atlantic group.

Greenberg's Arguments

Both Wolof and Serer-Sin belong to the West Sudanic family. If Fulani is shown to be closely related to Serer-Sin and Wolof, therefore, Fulani must be a member of the West Sudanic Family. He describes the relationship between Serer-Sin and Fulani with reference to the system of initial consonant alternation, derivative affixes and lexical resemblances.

-Initial Consonant Alternation
In Fulani, initial consonant alternations occur both in the noun and the verb.

-Nouns
The noun forms a set of twenty two classes: sixteen in the singular and six in the plural. In Serer-Sin, there are fourteen noun classes: ten in the singular; four in the plural. Greenberg argues that the Fulani system of initial consonant alternations is also obtained in Serer-Sin with a somewhat different form as illustrated in the following table.

BF	SS	SF	SN	FS	FF	FN
*g	k	g	ng	g	w/y	ng
*k	k	x	k	k	h	k
*d	t	r	nd	d	r	nd
*t	t	d	t	t	t	t
*l	l	l	l	l	l	l
*D	d	d	d	D	D	D

BF = base form; SS = Serer-Sin; SF = Serer Fricative; SN = Serer Nasalized; FS = Fulani Stop; FF = Fulani Fricative; FN = Fulani Nasalized

He argues that the correspondences that obtain in this table represent a sound proof of the genetic relationship between Fulani and Serer-Sin. Some of the correspondences described by Greenberg are problematic in certain respects. The correspondences cited by Greenberg are not always systematic observed from the following inconsistencies in Fula-Serer cognates (Sapir, 1971).

a1) w=v in war=var; but w=b in wind=bind; w=f in wam=fam; and w=g in worɓe=gor va

b1) y=y in yar=yer; but y=g in 3 pairs; while y=ng in yit=ngid

c1) h=x in several cases, but h=k in hoondu=kol

d1) r=r in several cases but also r=t

-Verbs

    Both Fulani and Serer-Sin have verb forms alternating between singular fricative and plural prenasalized. According to Greenberg, this highly unique alternation is only shared by Fulani and Serer-Sin. In this study of the system of alternation of initial consonants in Serer, Hestermann (1912) showed that Serer has an elaborate version of the very feature which had seemed peculiar to Fulani. Also, Klingenheben (1925) shows that the most unique and arbitrary feature of Fula, the consonant permutation system, is also matched point for point in the Biafada language spoken on the islands off the coast of Poruguese Guinea.

-Use of Derivative Affixes

    Another argument advanced by Greenberg to ascertain the genetic relationship between Serer-Sin and Fulani is that both languages have derivative affixes used with verbs which are very similar. For instance, the derivative affix {-AN} used to "perform an action to or for someone" is used in both languages; the derivative affix {-IR} used to "perform an action together with or by means of". Both Fula and Serer-Sin use exactly the same derivative affixes just mentioned.

-Lexical Resemblances

    Another argument suggested by Greenberg is the existence of a great number of lexical resemblances between Fula and Serer-Sin. He cites a great number of cognates between Serer and Fula.

    According to Greenberg, the initial consonant alternation and the similar use of an entire system of derivative affixes indicate the existence of a true genetic relationship between Fulani and Serer-Sin as these shared features cannot be accounted for by borrowing.

    Having analyzed the types of arguments used by Greenberg to justify his position, I provide additional evidence showing close relationship between Pulaar, Serer and Wolof.

Additional Features
-The Definite Article
   In all three languages, the definite article follows the noun even though
these determiners vary in form across these languages.

Fulani	Wolof	Serer-Sin
debbo o	jigeen ji	teo kha
woman the	woman the	woman the

-The Genitive
   The genitive is expressed exactly in the same fashion. That is, what is
owned, precedes the owner. For instance the phrase "Samba's horse" will
be expressed in all three in the same fashion as illustrated in the
following.

Serer-Sin	Wolof	Pulaar
pis Samba	fasu Samba	puccu Samba
horse Samba	horse Samba	horse Samba

-Position and Use of Adjectives
   In all three languages, the adjective follows the noun and modification
is indicated in the form of a relative clause as illustrated in the following.
Serer-Sin
teo a mos
woman who pretty   A pretty woman

Wolof
jigeen ju rafet
woman who pretty   A pretty woman

Pulaar
debbo jooddo
woman who pretty   A pretty woman

-Demonstratives
   In all three languages, the demonstrative is a variant of the definite
article of the noun class. In both Wolof and Serer, the demonstrative
follows the noun. In Pulaar, however, the demonstrative usually precedes
the noun.

Serer	Wolof	Pulaar
sa:x lene	rééw mii	ndii léydi
country this	country this	this country

-Comparison

The comparative operates also in the same fashion in all three languages. In these languages, the adverb for comparison occurs between the entities, objects, nouns being compared and the adjective is placed at the very end as indicated in the following data.

Wolof
Kumba moo gena Khadi rafet   Kumba is prettier than Khadi
kumba is more Khadi pretty

Serer
Kumba modjou Khadi mos   Kumba is prettier than Khadi
Kumba more Khadi pretty

Pulaar
Kumba buri Khadi yooɗde   Kumba is prettier than Khadi
Kumba more Khadi pretty

This data indicates that this type of comparison operates exactly in the same fashion in all three languages.

Conclusion

The controversy over the classification of Fulani has been analyzed and the various positions regarding this issue have been discussed. The arguments of the proponents of every position were analyzed and the value of these arguments were assessed. To this effect, Meinhof's position was rejected as his arguments were inconsistent with the facts of Pulaar as shown by the comparison of the characteristics of Hamitic languages and the facts of Pulaar. Westermann's position was in part supported by certain facts of Pulaar while many other aspects of Pulaar are inconsistent with his position. Both Meinhof and Westermann's arguments were assessed by Greenberg who showed that Meinhof and Westermann's positions are incorrect. Greenberg demonstrated the close relashionship of Fula to Serer-Sin and Wolof, which are West Atlantic languages, thereby demonstrating its own membership to the West Atlantic subfamily of Niger Congo. In addition, further aspects were described which are common to Pulaar, Wolof and Serer. Greenberg's position appears to be supported by the facts of Pulaar even though it was noted that there exist inconsistencies concerning consonant correspondences between Pulaar and Serer.

CHAPTER 2

SYLLABLE STRUCTURE CONSTRAINTS

Introduction

Syllable constituents may be represented in terms of binary branching diagrams with one obligatory constituent and two optional ones. The obligatory constituent, the Rhyme must dominate at least one V-slot on the skeletal tier. The optional constituents are the onset and coda. The Rhyme itself is divided into a Nucleus and a Coda.

The first constraints analyzed pertain to syllable structure as constraints on Pulaar syllable structure are responsible for various phonological processes that obtain in Pulaar.

Constraints on Pulaar syllable structure are analyzed in terms of restrictions in the distribution of syllables, the types of syllables allowed in the language, the types of consonant clusters permitted in word initial, medial and final positions. The separation of these levels is not intended to imply the absence of relationship among these levels as shown in the subsequent discussion.

The analysis of the constraints on Pulaar syllable structure, syllabification and resyllabification principles is done using various proposals. The proposals referred to relate to The Onset First Principle and The Well-formedness Conditions.

According to the Onset First Principle (Kahn 1976, Clements and Keyser 1983)

> Syllable-initial consonants are maximized to the extent consistent with the syllable structure conditions of the language in question. Syllable final consonants are maximized to the extent consistent with the syllable structure of the language in question.

According to The Well-formedness conditions

> Every segment in the melody is associated with at least one skeletal slot; every slot in the skeleton is associated with at least one segment in the melody; association lines do not cross.

The relationship that results from the above well-formedness conditions allows a one-to-many and a many-to-one association between segments and slots.

The theories utilized are the X-slot model of Levin (1985) and Kay and Lowenstamm (1986). In the X-slot model, syllabification rules are defined over the skeletal X-slots and phonological weight is determined by the presence or absence of two skeletal positions. Long vowels and long consonants are distinguished from short ones by the association of two successive skeletal positions. That is, short vowels and short consonants are associated with one skeletal position. Long vowels and long consonants are associated with two successive skeletal positions.

2.1 Levin's Approach

Levin (1985) views syllabification as an ordered set of structure building rules. She proposes the following syllabification rules and conditions in (2.1.1) through (2.1.4).

2.1.1 N"-projection

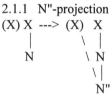

N the nucleus is the head of the syllable.

2.1.2 N'-Projection

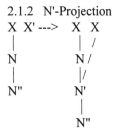

N'-projection is a language particular rule

2.1.3 Pre and Post Syllabification
The syllabification of pre and post nuclear consonants is done using rules of incorporation or rules of adjunction as in (2.1.3.1) and (2.1.3.2).
    2.1.3.1 Rules of Incorporation
    A. Into N"   B. Into N'

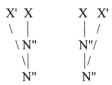

2.1.3.2 Rules of Adjunction
A. Initial   B. Final

```
X' X        X  X'
 \  |        |  /
  \ N"      N"/
   \|        |/
   N"        N"
```

Levin poses the following three conditions on syllable structure.
2.1.4 Conditions
2.1.4.1) An element of the category +N must be immediately dominated by N at every level. The category +N must be a syllable nucleus.

2.1.4.2) A long segment, that is, a single +N category matrix linked to two skeletal slots cannot be syllabified as two adjacent nuclei as illustrated in the following structures.

```
  [  ]        [  ]
   /\          /\
  X X  -->    X X
  |            \/
  N            N
```

The syllabification of segments immediately preceding the nucleus follows the universal syllabification of segments.

```
X  X  ---> X    X
|            \   |
N             \  N
               \ |
                \ N'
                 \|
                  N"
```

Before analyzing Pulaar syllable structure, an inventory of the segmental units is provided along with a discussion of their distribution.

2.2 Segment inventory

2.2.1 Consonants

	Bilab.	Lden.	Alv.	Pal.	Vel.	Glot.
Nasals	m		n	ñ	ŋ	
Prenasal.	ᵐb		ⁿd	ⁿj	ⁿg	
Plosives	p b		t d		k g	ʔ
Implosives	ɓ		ɗ	ʏ		
Fricatives		f	s			h
Affricates				c j		
Laterals			r			
			l			
Glides	w			y		

2.2.2 Vowels

i, ii	u, uu
e, ee	o, oo
	a, aa

2.2.3 Consonant and vowel distribution

2.2.3.1 Consonant Distribution

In Pulaar, all consonants can occur in word initial position. In word final position, all consonants can occur except the glottal stop /ʔ/.

2.2.3.1.1 Consonant clusters

Word Initial Word Medial Word Final
    C   CC   C

In word initial and final positions, no more than one consonant is allowed. A sequence of a nasal and a consonant is allowed in word initial and medial positions. In word initial position, the consonant following the nasal is always a voiced obstruent. In word medial position, not more than two consonants are allowed. In word medial position, the consonant following the nasal consonant can be voiced or voiceless. Prenasalized consonants behave like single consonants in Pulaar. Two arguments can be made to support this observation. First, consonant clusters are not allowed in word initial position. So, if prenasalized consonants occur in word initial position, they behave like single consonants instead of a sequence of two consonants. Second, a prenasalized consonant can be preceded by another consonant without leading to epenthesis as in (2.2.3.1.2).

2.2.3.1.2
kolndam   [kol^{n}dam]
morndolde   [mor^{n}dolde]

If prenasalized consonants behaved like two consonants, epenthesis would result since the language does not allow a three consonant cluster. Prenasalized consonants can occur word initially as in (2.2.3.1.3).

2.2.3.1.3
   mbaalu   [ᵐbaalu]
   ngalu   [ᵑgalu]
   ndiyam   [ⁿdiyam]

In this particular case, however, only voiced obstruents can follow the nasal consonants in word initial position. Even though a sequence of a nasal consonant followed by a voiceless obstruent is permitted in the language, this latter sequence is not allowed as the onset of a syllable as illustrated in (2.2.3.1.4).

2.2.3.1.4
      *mpade
      *nkaaye
      *ntaaniraado

Not every consonantal sequence is permitted. A detailed analysis of the constraints on consonant sequences is provided in the chapter dealing with gemination processes.

Even though the maximum sequence of consonants allowed is two, three consonant clusters occur in spoken Pulaar through the presence of intrusive consonants as in (2.2.3.1.5).

2.2.3.1.5
   wumtude [wumptude]
   humtude [humptude]

The forms in (2.2.3.1.5) are pronounced as a sequence of three consonant clusters because of the presence of the intrusive consonant.

2.2.3.2 Vowel Distribution

All vowels, long or short can occur in word initial, medial and final positions. The vowel /uu/ does not occur in word final position. Diphthongs, sequences of two perceptively different vowel sounds, do not occur in Pulaar. When a sequence of two perceptively different vowel sounds occurs across morpheme boundary, assimilation, glottal insertion or vowel deletion results.

In Pulaar, vowel length is phonemic as illustrated in the following contrasts.

hirde	vs.	hiirde
selde	vs.	seelde
surde	vs.	suurde
sorde	vs.	soorde
harde	vs.	haarde

2.3 Syllable Internal Structure

The syllable in Fula is restricted to the maximal structure in (2.3.1).
2.3.1

```
              σ
             / \
        Onset  Rime
      /        / \
     /     Nucleus Coda
    /        | \      |
  (X)       X(X)    (X)
```

Given the above structure, the syllable in Fula may consist of a null onset as in (2.3.2) and a null coda as in (2.3.3) or a null onset and coda as in (2.3.4).

2.3.2	2.3.3	2.3.4
ar	dara	a; oo

The nucleus, may consist of a short vowel as in (2.3.5) or a long vowel as in (2.3.6).

2.3.5	2.3.6
jal	jaal

When the nucleus consists of two vowels (long vowel), these must be vowels of the same quality. Not more than one consonant can be an onset.

A sequence of two consonants is not allowed in coda position. A syllable with two consonants in coda position is not well formed in Pulaar.

According to the syllable template in (2.3.1), the following surface syllable types are permitted in Fula.

2.3.7 Syllable Types

Syllable Type	Example
V	o
CV	mi
VC	on
CVC	dow
VV	oo
CVV	goo
VVC	aan
CVVC	kaaw

No other type of syllable is allowed in the language. The onset and coda are both optional constituents of the syllable in Fula. The Nucleus may have a short or a long vowel.

2.3.8 Syllable Combinations

All vowel initial syllables can precede consonant initial syllables as illustrated in the following.

Syllable types	*Examples*
V + CV	amo
V + CVC	ilam
V + CVV	alaa
V + CVVC	añaan
VV + CV	aaye
VV + CVV	aadee
VV + CVVC	aamiin
VV + CVC	ééɓól
VVC + CV	aawdi
VVC + CVC	aamtin
VVC + CVV	aastaa
VC + CV	asko
VC + CVC	awƴal
VC + CVV	ardii
VC + CVVC	éllééy

Vowel initial syllables are subject to various constraints and they cannot "freely" follow open syllables. The addition of a vowel initial syllable to the right of an open syllable can lead to vowel assimilation, vowel deletion or glottal insertion. All other syllable combinations are permitted in Pulaar even though some syllable combinations are more pervasive than others.

2.3.8.1 Monosyllabic Structures

The syllable structure of monosyllabic stems is illustrated in the section dealing with core syllables. Monosyllabic words are rather limited.

2.3.8.2 Disyllabic Structures

Disyllabic words have various structures some of which are illustrated in the following.

Syllable Types	Examples
V + CV	amo
V + CVC	ilam
V + CVV	idaa
V + CVVC	añaan
CV + CV	bala
CV + CVC	halal
CV + CVV	sahaa
CV + CVVC	Pulaar
VV + CV	aada
VV + CVV	aadéé
VV + CVVC	aamiin
VV + CVC	oolel
ⁿCVV + CV	mbaalu
CVV + CV	kaari
CVV + CVV	maakaa
CVV + CVVC	noogaas
CVV + CVC	baajol
VVC + CV	aawdi
VVC + CVC	óórgól
CVVC + CV	waalde
CVVC + VV	haal + ii
CVVC + VC	haal + an
CVVC + ⁿCVC	jaawngal

CVVC + CVC	maajgól
VC + V	am + i
VC + CV	ahde
VC + VV	ar + ii
VC + CVV	alfaa
VC + VC	as + ir
VC + CVC	awƴal
CVC + V	jal + i
CVC + CV	safde
CVC + VV	war + aa
CVC + CVVC	hamdaat
CVC + CVC	cólgól

Disyllabic words are more frequent than monosyllabic ones.

2.3.8.3 Trisyllabic Structures

Trisyllabic words can take various structures. Only a few of these structures are listed for illustration purposes.

Syllable Types	Examples
V CV CV	aduna
V CV CVC	asakal
CV CVC CV	nadorde
CV CV CV	ciluki

2.3.8.4 Tetrasyllabic Structures

Tetra syllabic words can have various structures. Only a few of these are listed for illustration purposes.

Syllable Types	Examples
CVC CV ⁿCVC CV	woɗ ɗo ndir de
CVV CV ⁿCV CV	haa ra ndu ru
CVV CV CVV CV	dóó ru maa ru
CVC CV CV CV	naj na ji lo

2.3.8.5 Pentasyllabic Structures

Pentasyllabic words are fairly common in Pulaar. Some pentasyllabic structures are illustrated in the following.

Syllable Types	*Examples*
CVC CV CV CVV CV	maw ni ki naa re
CVC CV CV CV CVC	ham ma ya ro yel
CVC CV CVV CV CVC	maw ni raa ge lam

It is argued in this study that vowel initial syllables are not preferred in this language. This argument rests on three important considerations. First, vowel initial suffixes are very rare in the language. Most suffixes are consonant initial suffixes. Second, the language does not allow a sequence of two perceptively different vowels. When a sequence of two perceptively different vowels is to result, assimilation, epenthesis, glottal insertion or glide formation occurs. Third, vowel initial words may surface with an initial glottal stop.

2.4 Constraints on Syllabification

The basic Pulaar syllable structure is CV(V)(C). The syllable in Pulaar can have no more than one consonantal segment in the onset position (except in the case of word initial geminate consonants) and not more than two consonants in coda position. No more than two vocalic segments (a long vowel) can occur in the nucleus.

Using Levin's X-theory model, Fula syllabification and resyllabification rules operate in the following order.

Assign a vocalic segment or segments to the nucleus as in (2.4.1).

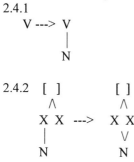

The syllabification in (2.4.1) and (2.4.2) follows from Conditions (2.1.4.1) and (2.1.4.2). The syllabification of pre and post nuclear consonants is done by means of incorporation as in (2.4.3.1) and (2.4.3.2).

2.4.3.1 Pre-nuclear incorporation

```
X'   X
 \   |
  \  N
   \ |
    \ N'
     \|
      N"
```

2.4.3.2 Post nuclear incorporation

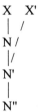

```
X  X'
|  /
N /
|/
N'
|
N"
```

The examples in (2.4.4) illustrate how the above rules and constraints operate.

2.4.4

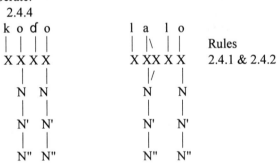

```
k o ɗ o              l a l o
| | | |              | |\ | |        Rules
X X X X              X XX X X        2.4.1 & 2.4.2
  |   |                |/    |
  N   N                N     N
  |   |                |     |
  N'  N'               N'    N'
  |   |                |     |
  N"  N"               N"    N"
```

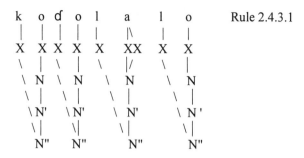

Rule 2.4.3.1

Having considered words containing open syllables, attention is directed to words with closed syllables such as "on" and "ɓalal" in (2.4.5).

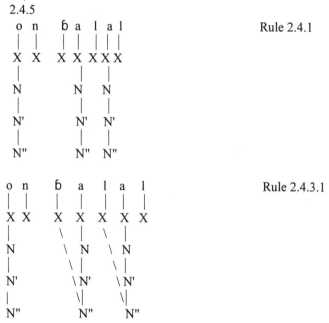

Rule 2.4.1

Rule 2.4.3.1

After the application of rules (2.4.1), (2.4.2) and (2.4.3.1), one X-slot remains unsyllabified. Using the post nuclear consonant incorporation rule (2.7.4.2), the unsyllabified X-slot and the consonant dominating it are attached to N'.

The derivations in (2.4.5) can then be completed using the post nuclear consonant incorporation rule as in (2.4.6).

2.4.6

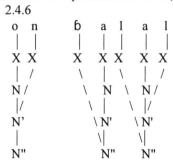

The adopted rules and constraints lead to the representations in (2.4.7).

2.4.7

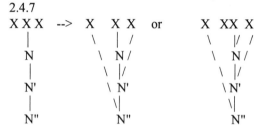

Having considered structures with open and closed syllables, the following discussion focuses on structures involving consonant clusters such as "helde". The application of syllable building rules (2.4.1), (2.4.2), (2.4.3.1) and (2.4.3.2) to this structure leads to the derivation of the structure in (2.4.7).

2.4.7

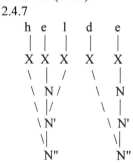

One might ask why can't [l] be syllabified with the following consonant instead? A number of reasons can be advanced to show that this latter position is not preferred. First, according to general universal principles, one expects the [l] to syllabify with the first syllable and the second consonant with the following vowel. Second, the grouping of the cluster [ld] to form the onset of the following syllable will violate Pulaar syllable structure constraints that do not allow more than one consonant to be an onset.

2.5 The Role of Epenthesis

A number of vowels function as cluster breakers that prevent the clustering of three consonant sequences as these are not allowed in the language. Vowels are also inserted to prevent an impermissible consonant cluster in word final position. The most common epenthetic vowel is /u/. The other vowels that serve to break three consonant clusters are /a/, /i/. These vowels occur between the second and third consonants of a three consonant cluster as in (2.5.1).

2.5.1

Root		Suffix	Surface Form
ust-	+	gol	ust-a-gol
nusk-	+	gol	nusk-u-gol
marɓ-	+	gol	marɓ-u-gol

In (2.5.1), the addition of the nominal suffix creates a sequence of three consonants. Fula, however does not permit a sequence of more than two consonants. This constraint forces the insertion of a vowel between the last two consonants. What follows shows how syllabification operates before the addition of the nominal suffixes "gol, gal". According to the syllable building rules, the structure of "nusk-" is (2.5.2).

2.5.2

One consonant is left stranded since a two consonant sequence is not allowed in coda position. The addition of the nominal suffix -gol to the root forces the insertion of a vowel to which the stranded consonant will syllabify. The previously stranded consonant becomes the onset of the syllable in which the inserted vowel is the nucleus. This resyllabification is illustrated in (2.5.3).

2.5.3

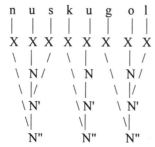

The epenthetic vowel /u/ can also serve to prevent the occurrence of an impermissible consonant cluster in word final position.

2.6 Rule Ordering

Some ordering is required for the proposed syllabification rules. Overall, three syllable building rules were proposed for Fula syllabification and resyllabification processes. These rules must be applied in the following order to avoid incorrect syllabification. Rule (2.4.1) applies first, followed by rule (2.4.3.1) which is then followed by rule (2.4.3.2). If this order is not followed, incorrect syllabification results as in (2.6.1).

2.6.1

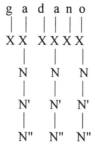

The application of rule (2.4.3.2) before rule (2.4.3.1), yields the structure in (2.6.2).

2.6.2

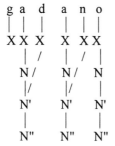

The application of rule (2.4.3.1) results in the derivations in (2.6.3).

2.6.3

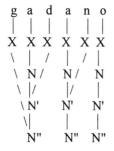

Two onsetless syllables appear in (2.6.3). The syllabification in (2.6.3) does not follow general universal principles of syllabification.

Conclusion

In this chapter, an analysis of constraints on Fula syllabification and resyllabification principles was proposed that accounts for the processes involved. Various proposals such as the onset first principle and the well formedness conditions were used, conditions that are useful for Pulaar syllabification and resyllabification processes.

CHAPTER 3

GEMINATION CONSTRAINTS

Introduction

Various types of gemination processes result, in general, from constraints on consonantal sequences allowed by the language and the types of consonants that can be geminated.

This chapter focuses on three types of gemination processes that obtain in Pulaar. The first gemination process is triggered by the addition of consonant initial suffixes. This type of gemination process is not unidirectional as is generally claimed. The spreading can take the left to right direction or the right to left direction. This kind of gemination is widely spread in the language and various consonants trigger or undergo this process. The second gemination process results from the addition of certain vowel initial suffixes. The third type of gemination occurs in word initial position. This type of gemination is triggered by the presence of word medial geminates.

It is argued in this study that some geminates are underlying and others are not. Arguments to this effect are provided in due course. Geminates, in general, occur in word initial and medial positions. This constraint is due to the fact that consonant clusters are not allowed in ord initial and final positions.

This section addresses various constraints on gemination processes, explains the motivations behind these constraints and shows how the language repairs and prevents potential violations of these constraints.

Before analyzing Pulaar gemination processes, a brief discussion of how geminates are represented in the X-slot is provided.

In X-theory, the geminate is associated with two X-slots. The first is the coda of the first syllable and the second the onset of the second syllable. Using the X-slot model, tautomorphemic geminates in Pulaar can have the following representation.

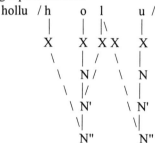

The analysis of gemination processes and constraints adopted here shows the inadequacies of previous analyses of gemination in Pulaar by Paradis (1992) and Bakovic (1995).

3.1 Previous Analyses

3.1.1 Paradis' Analysis
Paradis (1992) remarks that "the absence of the geminate ŋŋ must be seen as an accidental gap ..."

Paradis suggests a phonemic constraint on geminates and a hardening rule (3.1.2).

   3.1.2
   -phonemic constraint on geminate consonants

        X   X
         \ /
          C
     [-continuant]

She indicates that "when a continuant consonant must geminate, it is occlusivized by the repair strategy..." in (3.1.3).

3.1.3

-Occlusivization Repair Strategy

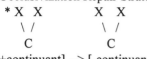

```
 * X   X        X   X
   \ /          \ /
    C            C
```

[+continuant] --> [-continuant]

Paradis indicates that gemination in Pulaar is triggered by ɗV markers and she proposes the following gemination rule (3.1.4).

3.1.4

Gemination Rule Stratum I

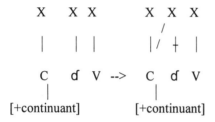

```
 X   X X       X  X  X
                  /
 |   | |       |/ + |


 C   ɗ V -->   C  ɗ  V
 |             |
[+continuant]   [+continuant]
```

The analysis proposed here differs from this proposal in at least three important respects. First, ɗV markers are used to mark plural nominals. One possible implication of her proposal is that singular nouns do not geminate since they do not use ɗV markers in their singular forms. However, there are singular nominals with geminate consonants as in (3.1.5).

3.1.5

ɓoodde	[ɓoodde]
wuddu	[wuddu]
ladde	[ladde]

These instances clearly represent counter examples to the implications of her proposal. Second, the use of ɗV markers excludes gemination in verbal complexes. Verbal complexes do not carry the ɗV markers. So if gemination is triggered only by ɗV markers, verbal complexes are not expected to geminate since they do not take ɗV markers. Verbal complexes can have geminates as in (3.1.6).

3.1.6
hóccu   [hóccu]
ɗójju   [ɗɗójju]
Ɣéttu   [ƔƔéttu]
móƔƔu   [mmóƔƔu]
héédnude   [héénnude]

Third, in many instances, gemination fails to apply despite the presence of ɗV markers as in (3.1.7).

3.1.7
ɓale   ɗe   [ɓale ɗe]
gite   ɗe   [gite ɗe]
nate   ɗe   [nate ɗe]
jale   ɗe   [jale ɗe]
maje   ɗe   [maje ɗe]

Paradis indicates that /ñ, r, w, y/ do not have geminate counterparts. Actually, except /r/, all these consonants have geminate counterparts. She also indicates that gemination is triggered by ɗV markers and cites exceptions to her gemination rule.

The adopted analysis shows that instances previously considered exceptions to gemination rules are not exceptions. Paradis lists exceptions to her gemination rule, some of which are reproduced in (3.1.8).

3.1.8
Plural forms
new-e   (ɗe)
low-e   (ɗe)
giy-e   (ɗe)
ges-e   (ɗe)

These are not exceptions to the analysis proposed here for a number of reasons. First, in Pulaar, there are two types of /w/. One is underlying and the other one is derived. As far as nouns are concerned, /w/ is never geminated; neither is /y/ except in few proper names and interjections. The /w, s, y/ in her examples do not alternate from singular to plural, thus strongly suggesting that these root final consonants are underlying. The singular forms of the data in (3.1.8) are illustrated in (3.1.9).

3.1.9
Singular forms
new-re (nde)
low-re (nde)
giy-al (ngal)
nges-a (ba)

Contrary to what obtains in nominal complexes, /w/ and /y/ can geminate in verbal complexes as in (3.1.10).

3.1.10

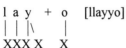

[llayyo]

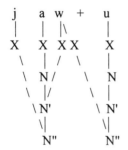

[jjawwu]

The examples in (3.1.10) clearly indicate that both /y/ and /w/ can geminate. Furthermore, the analysis adopted in this study differs from Paradis (1992) in that she refers to a constraint on geminate sequences according to which "geminate consonants in Pulaar cannot be preceded by a long vowel". This claim is not supported by the type of data in (3.1.11).

3.1.11

ɓoodde
kaaddi
naatde [naadde]
fooɗde [foodde]

3.1.2 Bakovic's Analysis

Bakovic (1995) provides an analysis of gemination in Pulaar using the Optimality Theory approach (Prince and Smolensky 1993). His analysis, based on Paradis (1992) suffers from the shortcomings pertaining to the source.

3.2) Geminate Consonant Types

Prior to analyzing the type of gemination processes that obtain in Pulaar, examples of the types of consonantal segments that can be geminated in Pulaar are provided. Except s, r, f, and h, all single consonants in Fula have geminate counterparts as illustrated in (3.2.1).

3.2.1

Geminate type	Example
ll	hóll-u
tt	yétt-u
dd	nódd-u
ɗɗ	faɗɗ-u
nn	bónn-u
mm	timm-u
ŋŋ	kaŋŋe
ññ	sóññ-u
cc	hocc-u
jj	wujj-u
bb	ubb-u
ɓɓ	haɓɓ-u
kk	rókk-u

gg	rugg-u
pp	happ-u
ɤɤ	móɤɤ-u
yy	sayy-o
ww	jaww-u

Instances where /r/ is geminated are uncommon. Only one instance (borrowed word) was found where /r/ is geminated as in (3.2.2)

3.2.2   qirraade

The fact that /r/ does not geminate is attributed to an accidental gap in Pulaar. The other three consonants that do not geminate are all [-voice +continuant]. In Pulaar [-voice + continuant] consonants do not have geminate counterparts. The behavior of these consonants when they occur in a position that satisfies the conditions for gemination is addressed in the relevant section. Some geminates are viewed as underlying while others are not. Such an important generalization is crucial ;in the analysis of gemination processes in Pulaar. The test used to determine whether a geminate is underlying rests on whether there is an alternation between the singular and plural forms of the nominal or verbal complexes. Plurality is generally marked in two different ways. It can be marked by the addition of a plural suffix or by the alternation of the first consonant.

The data in (3.2.3) illustrates instances where plurality is marked by suffixation. The plural suffix is "-ji". The vowel preceding the plural suffix is always long.

3.2.3
Sing.	Plur.
lamba	lambaaji
mata	mataaji
naange	naangééji
ñalawma	ñalawmaaji
tata	tataaji
mbandu	mbanduuji

It appears as if stems beginning with the sonorants [m, n, ñ, ŋ, l], the implosives [ɓ,ɗ,ʏ], voiced obstruents [b, d, j, g,] and voiceless obstruents [p, t, k, c] and prenasalized consonants which are not derived do not alternate from singular to plural. Their plural is generally marked by the addition of a plural suffix.

Other consonantal segments behave differently in the way plurality is marked. The data in (3.2.4) illustrates plurality marked by initial consonant alternation.

3.2.4

Sing.	Plur.
walabo	balabe
réédu	déédi
yeeso	jeese
sekko	cekke
hello	kelle
njamndi	jamɗe
mbaalu	baali
ndamndi	damɗi
ngaska	gasɗe

It appears as if stems beginning with w, r, y, f, s, h, alternate from singular to plural. The chart in (3.2.5) is provided to illustrate the consonant alternation between singular and plural forms (Sylla 1982).

3.2.5

sing.	f	s	h	r	w	ʔ	y
	|	|	|	|	| \ | / |
plur.	p	c	k	d	b	g	j
	|	|	|	|	| | |
plur. dim.	p	c	k	nd	mb	ng	nj

Both /w/ and /y/ have more than one alternation as illustrated in the following.

wudere	-->	gude	ngudon
wowru	-->	boɓi	mboɓon
yertere	-->	gerte	ngerton
abbere	-->	gabbe	ngabbon

Despite the fact that the above remarks help to capture important generalizations, many exceptions can be found. These exceptions are addressed only if relevant to the motivations and concerns of this study.

Geminates that do not alternate in the singular and plural forms of
nominal or verbal complexes are viewed as underlying geminates as in
(3.2.6).

3.2.6
Nominal complexes
Singular   Plural

3.2.6.1
lell-a   léll-i
mall-ol   mall-i

3.2.6.2
mol-a   mol-i
jal-o   jal-e
pal-al   pal-e

3.2.6.3
léw-ru   lébb-i
fów-ru   póbb-i
hóf-ru   kópp-i
nóf-ru   nópp-i
gujj-o   wuy-be

Where some alternation is involved in the singular and plural forms of
the noun complex, the type of geminates that are formed are not viewed
as "underlying". Such data is illustrated in (3.2.6.3).
Only the vowels -I and -e occur in plural nominals. The quality of the
word final vowel is generally similar to that of the vowel of the noun class
marker.
In (3.2.6.3) the following alternations are observed.

w   -   b
f   -   p
y   -   j

The problem that arises with these alternations is to determine which
segments are underlying. Are /w, f, y/ underlying or are /b, p, j/
underlying? All possibilities are explored to assess the adequacy of every
alternative in the section concerning gemination from vowel initial
suffixation.

Having discussed how plurality is marked in nominal complexes, the next focus is on verbal complexes.

Verbal Complexes

The verb in Pulaar is composed of a root followed by different suffixes. Plurality in verbal complexes is essentially marked by initial consonant alternation. The consonants that alternate in nominal complexes also alternate in verbal complexes. Those that do not alternate in nominal complexes will not alternate in verbal complexes. The data in (3.2.7) illustrates some types of suffixation in verbal complexes (3.2.7).

3.2.7
hel-de	"to break"
hel-aa	"is broken"
hél-i	"broke"

"hel-" is the root; "de" is the infinitival suffix; "-aa" is a passive suffix; "-i" is a present tense marker.

As far as verbal complexes are concerned, many types of underlying geminates can be found. The same alternation test used for nominals to determine whether a geminate is underlying is utilized as in (3.2.7.1) and (3.2.7.2).

3.2.7.1		3.2.7.2	
Geminates		*Non geminates*	
sing.	plural	sing.	plural
sell-i	cell-i	sel-i	cel-i
sokk-i	cokk-i	sok-i	cok-i

The data in (3.2.7.1) and (3.2.7.2) illustrates the absence of alternation in verbal complexes. That is, geminates in the singular form of a verb remain geminates in the plural form of the verb. Non geminates in the singular form of verbs remain non geminates in the plural form of the verb.

The above data suggests that the underlying forms of the verbs are #sell-# for "sell-i" and #sel-# for "sel-i".

This alternation test shows the difference that between underlying and non-underlying geminates.

In addition to the underlying geminates in nominal complexes, other geminates are formed that are not viewed as "underlying". These geminates are viewed as non underlying because there is an alternation between the singular and the plural forms of these noun complexes.

This type of data is illustrated in (3.2.7.3).

3.2.7.3

Singular	Plural
sof-ru	copp-i
lew-ru	lebb-i

Since these geminates are not underlying, their formation must be triggered by some process. It is argued that gemination in Pulpar is triggered by suffixation and the need to respect the constraints imposed by the language. Two types of suffixes are involved in these types of gemination processes. One type of suffix is consonant initial. The other type is a surface vowel initial suffix. It is argued in this study that vowel initial suffixes had consonants in their earlier forms which where dropped during the evolutionary process of the language. Gemination in Pulpar operates like a repair strategy by providing vowel initial suffixes with an onset and by preventing impermissible consonant sequences.

With these preliminary remarks, the following discussion focuses on the examination of Pulpar gemination processes. The analysis focuses on gemination resulting from consonant assimilation and gemination from vowel initial suffixation.

3.3 Gemination Processes

3.3.1 Consonant Assimilation

The addition of suffixes to certain stems can lead to gemination in Pulpar. The suffixes analyzed here are the causative suffix "n", the infinitive suffix "de", the relative suffix "ɗo" and the reversive suffix "t". A sample of the data analyzed is presented, followed by generalizations and then the application of the proposed analysis. The data in (3.3.1.1) illustrates instances where assimilation does not occur.

3.3.1.1

hul	+	n	+	u		[hulnu]
has	+	n	+	u		[hasnu]
aaɓ	+	n	+	u		[aaɓnu]
soof	+	n	+	u		[sóófnu]
dog	+	n	+	u		[dógnu]
yim	+	n	+	u		[yimnu]
am	+	n	+	u		[amnu]
yar	+	n	+	u		[yarnu]

waaw	+	n	+	u	[waawnu]
woy	+	n	+	u	[wóynu]
wel	+	de			[welde]
hel	+	de			[helde]
wis	+	de			[wisde]
hes	+	de			[hesde]
heɓ	+	de			[heɓde]
laaɓ	+	de			[laaɓde]
saaf	+	de			[saafde]
sef	+	de			[sefde]
tag	+	de			[tagde]
dog	+	de			[dogde]
mah	+	de			[mahde/maade]
saak	+	de			[saakde]
sok	+	de			[sokde]
ham	+	de			[hamde]
rem	+	de			[remde]
hon	+	de			[honde]
yon	+	de			[yonde]
hor	+	de			[horde]
moor	+	de			[moorde]
sow	+	de			[sowde]
sew	+	de			[sewde]
woy	+	de			[woyde]
maay	+	de			[maayde]
laaɓ	+	ɗo			[laaɓɗo]
leef	+	ɗo			[leefɗo]
dog	+	ɗo			[dogɗo]
jook	+	ɗo			[jookɗo]
jol	+	ɗo			[jolɗo]
mem	+	ɗo			[memɗo]
bon	+	ɗo			[bonɗo]
tir	+	ɗo			[tirɗo]
tey	+	ɗo			[teyɗo]
naw	+	ɗo			[nawɗo]
hol	+	t	+	i	[holti]
soof	+	t	+	i	[soofti]
yar	+	t	+	i	[yarti]
hel	+	t	+	i	[helti]
heɓ	+	t	+	i	[heɓti]

In (3.3.1.1) the addition of any of the above suffixes does not result in any change of any of the adjacent consonants. The data in (3.3.1.2) illustrates instances involving the optional deletion of "h" before another consonant.

3.3.1.2

loh	+ n + u	[lóhnu] / [lóónu]
mah	+ n + u	[mahnu] / [maanu]
mah	+ do	[mahdo] / [maado]
sah	+ de	[sahde] / [saade]
mah	+ t + i	[mahti] / [maati]

In (3.3.1.2) two observations can be made. The addition of the suffixes may or may not lead to any change of any of the adjacent consonants. Optionally, the addition of these suffixes can result in the deletion of the stem final consonant and the lengthening of the vowel preceding it. This consonant deletion can be captured by the rule in (3.3.1.3).

3.3.1.3

   h ---> ø / - c

The following analysis is applied to these optional processes (3.3.1.4).
3.3.1.4
-Delinking
-Spreading (compensatory lengthening)

The proposed analysis is applied to determine its adequacy for the cases in (3.3.1.5)

   l o h + n u ----> [loonu]

Delinking leaves an empty X-slot as in (3.3.1.6).
3.3.1.6

```
l  o  h   n  u
|  |  +   |  |
X  X  X   X  X
```

Vowel lengthening: the empty X-slot is filled by leftward spreading of the stem vowel as in (3.3.1.7).
3.3.1.7

```
l  o    n  u
|  | ·.  |  |
X  X  X  X  X
```

Additional data is presented in (3.3.1.8) to determine the adequacy of the proposed analysis.

3.3.1.8

mut	+	n + u	[munnu]
suut	+	n + u	[suunnu]
sood	+	n + u	[sóónnu]
wood	+	n + u	[wóónnu]
hoɗ	+	de	[hodde]
haɗ	+	de	[hadde]
waat	+	de	[waadde]
fot	+	de	[fodde]
naat	+	ɗo	[naadɗo]
laad	+	ɗo	[laadɗo]
waɗ	+	t + u	[watti]
Sood	+	t + i	[sooti]

In (3.3.1.8) two observations can be made. The stem final consonant is assimilated and the suffix consonant is geminated. The proposed analysis is applied to this set of data to determine the adequacy of the analysis.

m u t + n u ---> [munnu]

-Delinking leaves an empty X-slot as in (3.3.1.9).
3.3.1.9

```
m u t n u ---> m u     n u
| | ┼ | |       | |     | |
X X X X X       X X X X X
```

-Spreading of the suffix consonant fills the empty X-slot and leads to gemination as in (3.3.1.10).
3.3.1.10

```
m u     n u
| |  /  | |
X X X X X
```

In X-Theory, this kind of gemination can be captured by the following (3.3.1.11).

3.3.1.11

The proposed analysis appears to be adequate in that it accounts for the data presented so far. Additional data is presented in (3.3.1.12) to further test this analysis.

3.3.1.12

Stem		Suffix		Phonetic Form
taʕ	+	ɗo	-->	[taʕʕo]
mooʕ	+	ɗo	-->	[mooʕʕo]
ʕoʕ	+	ɗo	-->	[ʕoʕʕo]
deeʕ	+	ɗo	-->	[deeʕʕo]
haac	+	t + i	-->	[haacci]

In (3.3.1.12), the suffix consonant undergoes assimilation. The stem final consonant is geminated. The proposed analysis is applied to the data in (3.3.1.12).

-Delinking leaves an empty X-slot as in (3.3.1.13).

3.3.1.13

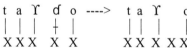

-Spreading: rightward spreading occurs, filling the empty X-slot thus resulting in gemination as in (3.3.1.14).

3.3.1.14

This type of gemination can be represented by the following rule (3.3.1.15)

3.3.1.15

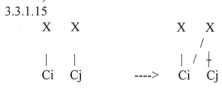

Condition Ci = ƴ   Cj = ɗ

Rightward spreading can also occur in instances that do not involve implosives as illustrated by the data in (3.3.1.16).

3.3.1.16

stem		inf. suf.	surface form
fij	+	de	[fijje]
hij	+	de	[hijje]
moj	+	de	[mojje]

Delinking leaves an empty X-slot as in (3.3.1.17).

3.3.1.17

Spreading: rightward spreading occurs, filling the empty X-slot thus resulting in gemination as in (3.3.1.18).

3.3.1.18

Unlike what obtains in the gemination processes analyzed so far in this section concerning assimilation processes, the spreading in (3.3.1.12) and (3.3.1.16) is from right to left and the segment that is deleted is the second segment contrary to a claim by Paradis (1986a) according to which "It is always the first consonant of a consonant cluster that is deleted..."

The proposed analysis is tested against additional data in (3.3.1.19).

3.3.1.19

maaj	+	n + u	[maaññu]
yaaj	+	n + u	[yaaññu]
weej	+	n + u	[wééññu]
wooc	+	de	[woojje]
haac	+	de	[haajje]
heʕ	+	de	[hejje]
waaʕ	+	de	[waajje]
maaj	+	ɗo	[maaYYo]
waaʕ	+	t + i	[waacci]

In (3.3.1.19), gemination occurs. This gemination process is somewhat different from the ones analyzed so far. In previous instances involving assimilation, after delinking, the features of one segment spread onto the X-slot of the stem final consonant or the suffix initial X-slot. The features of the segment where spreading originates are not affected at all. That is, the particular segment does not lose its features. In (3.3.1.19) a different process occurs. After gemination we get the form [maaññu] not [maannu] as expected. When viewed like the usual spreading of features to a slot which has become vacant because of delinking, this type of gemination will not be accounted for.

The delinking of the stem final consonant results in the geminate in (3.3.1.20).

3.3.1.20

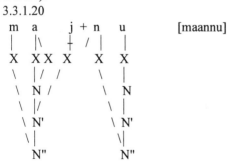

[maannu]

The delinking of the suffix initial consonant yields the geminate in (3.3.1.21)

3.3.1.21

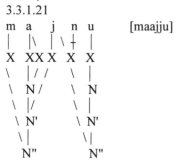

[maajju]

The forms in (3.3.1.20) and (3.3.1.21) are different from the surface forms in (13.5). If the delinking process is not invoked, one cannot explain why spreading has to occur since there is no empty slot at all. It is argued here that delinking occurs first because without delinking, there is no motivation for spreading to occur. However, the palatal features of the delinked element remain "floating" thus causing the dental nasal consonant suffix to surface as a palatal nasal. If the palatal features did not remain "floating" the palatalization of the dental nasal cannot be accounted. This assimilation is reciprocal between the segments in question.

The proposed analysis accounts for all the gemination processes involving gemination from consonant assimilation. The following analysis provides explanations underlying these gemination processes and the components of the analysis that have been proposed.

It is argued that gemination from consonant assimilation is triggered by the fact that certain coronal consonant sequences are not allowed in Pulpar. Whenever an impermissible sequence is to result from the juxtaposition of certain elements, one of the consonants assimilates to the other consonant. The type of assimilation that obtains generally involves total assimilation, thus indicating why delinking is invoked. Delinking triggers spreading onto the empty slot. As shown above, spreading is not unidirectional. It can be from left to right of from right to left.

All instances of gemination resulting from consonant assimilation have been analyzed and accounted for. Three major processes were analyzed. The first involves total assimilation of the stem final consonant. The second involves total assimilation of the suffix consonant. The third process involves reciprocal assimilation.

Following the analysis of consonant initial gemination, the next section focuses on gemination processes involving vowel initial suffixes.

3.3.2 *Vowel Initial Suffixation*

Certain geminates are viewed as underlying and others are not viewed as underlying geminates. The alternation test previously used serves to determine whether a geminate is underlying. That is where there is no alternation between singular and plural as far as geminates are concerned, the gemination involved is viewed as underlying. The data in (3.3.2.1) illustrates underlying geminates.

3.3.2.1

bajj	+	-o	[bajjo]
ball	+	-a	[balla]
moʕʕ	+	-o	[moʕʕo]
lett	+	-o	[letto]
ɗojj	+	-o	[ɗojjo]

The representation of these underlying geminates in X-theory is illustrated in (3.3.2.2).

3.3.2.2

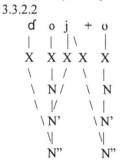

The forms in (3.3.2.1) are geminates in their underlying forms. Therefore, the need to invoke a trigger for these underlying geminates does not arise.

Unlike the -o and -a suffixes, two vowel initial suffixes lead to gemination. These vowel initial suffixes are -in and -i. -in is the causative suffix and -i is a plural marker.

First, the analysis will focus on the causative suffix. Data illustrating the addition of the causative suffix "-in" is presented in (3.3.2.3).

3.3.2.3

waal	+	-in	[wallin]
laam	+	-in	[lammin]
ñaam	+	-in	[ñammin]
saam	+	-in	[sammin]
leem	+	-in	[lémmin]

The addition of the causative suffix leads to gemination and the previously long vowel is shortened. The previously long vowel is shortened only before a final heavy syllable. According to Paradis and Prunet (1989), the causative suffix is {-n} and /i/ is a vowel that is inserted to break a three consonant cluster. The analysis that is proposed here does not view {-n} only as the causative suffix.

If the causative suffix is {-n} then we are dealing with an instance of vowel insertion which is supported by two observations. The first observation is that the insertion of /i/ is to prevent the presence of a three consonant cluster, a sequence that is not allowed in the language. In this case, insertion follows gemination. The second observation is that /i/ occurs in an environment where insertion is expected. i.e. between the last two consonants of a three consonant cluster. Two problems arise if we consider the causative suffix to be {-n}. First, /i/ is not the vowel that is generally inserted to break a three consonant cluster in verbal complexes as in (3.3.2.4).

3.3.2.4

halk-u-de
losk-u-de

The vowel /u/ in the above data is an epenthetic vowel.

Besides, if the form of the causative suffix is "-n", one cannot account for the gemination that resulted from the addition of this suffix to the stem. As explained earlier, gemination from consonant assimilation occurs to prevent an impermissible consonant cluster. The clusters /mn/, /ln/, /wn/, /sn/ are permissible clusters as in (3.3.2.5).

3.3.2.5

amnude
haalnude
séwnude
hasnude

If {-n} is the causative suffix, there is no motivation for gemination to occur. Besides, various forms take both {-n} and {-in} suffixes as in (3.3.2.6).

3.3.2.6

naat	+	in	--->	[naattin]
naat	+	n + u	--->	[naannu]
deeɣ	+	n + u	--->	[deeññu]
deeɣ	+	in	--->	[deɣɣin]

In (15.2) the suffixes {-n} and {-in} can both occur with the same root with different meanings. This situation is not expected if we are dealing with the same suffix. Therefore the {-n} and {-in} suffixes are viewed as different suffixes.

Since there is no motivation for gemination to occur when {-n} alone is viewed as the causative suffix, the other alternative which considers the causative suffix to be {-in} is explored.

As it stands, the proposed analysis will not account for the forms in (3.3.2.3). In previous instances dealing with gemination resulting from assimilation, the deletion of one of the consonants leads to the presence of an empty X-slot. Spreading fills the empty X-slot, thus leading to gemination. However, in these instances, no assimilation occurs for spreading to be invoked. Spreading cannot occur without the presence of an empty X-slot. For this reason, the causative suffix is postulated to have an apparently underlying featureless empty X-slot represented in (3.3.2.7).

3.3.2.7

In order to determine the adequacy of the proposed analysis, it is tested against this new set of data.

```
l  e   m + i  n    [léémmin]
|  |\  |   |  |
X  X X X   X X X
```

-Delinking: not applicable
-Spreading onto the empty X-slot

```
l   e   m    i n
|   |\  |\   | |
X X X X X X X
```

This type of gemination can be captured by either of the following gemination rules (3.3.2.8).

3.3.2.8

```
- [ F ]        [ F ]
   |            /\
   X   --->    X X / -] + -in

- X            X X
  |            | |
  C   --->     C C / -] + -in
```

As formulated, the analysis will not adequately account for the data in (15.0). This derived form [léémmin] is not the surface form. In order to account for the data in (3.3.2.3), the addition of another component (vowel shortening) to the analysis is required. This vowel shortening rule is formulated in (3.3.2.9).

3.3.2.9

```
                    σ
   V   --->   V / - / \
   /\         |   X X
  X X         X
```

The application of this vowel shortening rule yields the correct output [lémmin].

Prunet and Tellier (1984) claim that (C)VC suffixes do not shorten long vowels in word initial position when they indicate that "... this alternation never affects a vowel in the first syllable of the stem/root:..."

The type of data listed in (3.3.2.3) and analyzed through (3.3.2.9) indicates that this vowel shortening rule can also apply to certain instances with a long vowel in word initial position.

This vowel shortening also supports our analysis which considers {-in} as the suffix since the particular vowel shortening occurs only in the presence of a (C)VC or (C)VV suffix.

The other type of vowel initial suffix that causes gemination is the nominal plural suffix -I. In general, this plural suffix causes only the gemination of [+ continuants]. This vowel initial suffix is assumed to have the representation in (3.3.2.10).

3.3.2.10

i
|
X X

The adequacy of the proposed analysis is tested against additional data in (3.3.2.11) and (3.3.2.12).

3.3.2.11	3.3.2.12
singular	plural
a)	a')
sóf-ru	cópp-i
nóf-ru	nópp-i
hóf-ru	kópp-i
b)	b')
saw-ru	cabb-i
léw-ru	lébb-i
fów-ru	póbb-i
c)	c')
dóy-ru	dójj-i

As formulated, the analysis will not account for the data in (3.3.2.11) and (3.3.2.12) even though the plural suffix is assumed to have an empty X-slot. The analysis predicts the forms in (3.3.2.13).

3.3.2.13

*/cóffi; nóffi; dóyyi/.

In order to account for these cases, another component (consonant hardening) needs to be added to the analysis. Consonant hardening affects only the following consonants: s, f, h, w, y. The consonants /s, f, h/ do not geminate in Pulpar. That is, the forms /*ss, *ff, *hh/ do not occur in the language. Since these consonants do not have geminate forms, they are changed into segments that are allowed to geminate when the conditions for gemination are satisfied. The candidates for /s/ and /f/ could be their voiced counterparts /z/ and /v/ respectively. These, however, do not occur in the language. The /*yy, *ww/ do not occur in nominal complexes even though these last two occur in verbal complexes. These segments are therefore changed into forms that can be geminated. So s --> c, f --> p, h --> k, w --> b, y --> j.

Since this chapter deals with gemination, the hardening of /s, f, h, w, y/ is addressed only when relevant to gemination. Consonant hardening can be captured by the rule in (3.3.2.14).

3.3.2.14

```
α  ---->  β    / - ] + -i
/ \       / \
X X      X X
```

The analysis of the data in (3.3.2.11) and (3.3.2.12) requires various proposals. According to one proposal #nop# in (a), #leb# in (b), #ɗóy# in (c) are the underlying forms of the stems. The addition of the plural nominal suffix triggers gemination as the last consonant of the root stem links to the featureless empty X-slot of the suffix as illustrated in (3.3.2.15).

3.3.2.15

```
n o p     i
| | |\    |
XXX X   X
```

Another alternative is to view the singular forms as underlying. In this case the underlying form of the stem is #sof-#. As mentioned earlier, the segment /f/ does not have a geminate counterpart. The problem that arises relates to determining how the stem final segment becomes realized as /p/ in its surface form. One approach may invoke a process of hardening whereby /f/ changes into /p/, /w/ into /b/ and /y/ into /j/ when they occur in a gemination environment. These processes are illustrated in the following derivation.

```
# sof # + i
s  o  f  +  i
|  |  |     |
X  X  X   X X
```

Rightward spreading occurs filling the empty X-slot and leading to gemination as illustrated in the following derivation.

```
s  o  f  +  i
|  |  | \    |
X  X  X  X
```

Consonant hardening occurs changing "ff" into "pp" and the following structure is derived.

[c o p p i]

The first proposal seems to follow the general gemination process whereby the stem final consonant links to the empty featureless X-slot of the vowel initial suffix. The rule changing /f, w, y/ to /p,b,j/ respectively is also a plausible phonological operation. The second alternative also leads to gemination. The conditions that trigger the hardening of the stem final consonant still remain to be determined. Instances where consonant hardening does not occur are illustrated in (3.3.2.16).

3.3.2.16

Sing.dim. / augment.		Plur. dim.
cóf-él /	cof-al	cof-on
nóf-él /	nof-al	nof-on
caw-él /	caw-al	caw-on
léw-él /	lew-al	
(léwléwél) /	(lewlewal)	lewlew-on

The addition of the singular diminutive suffix (-el), the singular augmentative suffix (-al) and the plural diminutive suffix (-on) leaves the [+cont.] forms unaltered. The only instances where the [-cont.] forms are present are the geminated cases. Therefore, the [+cont.] forms can be viewed as underlying.

A third alternative can view the plural forms as underlying and the singular ones as derived. In this case, a weakening or softening rule is needed that changes the root final obstruents into /f/, /s/, /y/ or /w/. This third alternative is not supported by the data in (3.3.2.16).

A fourth alternative may analyze the stem final consonant as an abstract segment different from any of the forms that appear on surface either in the singular or plural forms. This abstract underlying form surfaces into a segment allowed to geminate when it appears in a gemination environment. In the singular form of the nominal complex, this abstract form surfaces in various forms. If the stem final abstract underlying segment is voiced in its singular form, the plural counterpart is voiced and vice versa. If it is voiceless, the plural counterpart is voiceless. There appears to be a correlation between the stem final consonant in the singular and the stem final consonant in the plural as far as voicing is concerned. This third alternative involving an abstract underlying segment can be represented in (3.3.2.17)

```
        3.3.2.17
 n  o  p   i
 |  |  |\  |
 X X  X - X X      X    --->    XX /-
```

This fourth alternative is rather appealing and it does not suffer from the additional stipulations that had to be invoked with the other alternatives.

As formulated the proposed analysis accounts for all the gemination processes presented so far. The proposed analysis is reiterated in (3.3.2.18).

    3.3.2.1.8
    -Delinking
    -Spreading (gemination/vowel lengthening)
    -Vowel shortening
    -Consonant hardening

Word initial gemination in Pulpar is the subject of the next section.

3.3.3 Word Initial Gemination

Word initial geminates have been documented for Luganda and Ponapeian (Hayes, 1989). In Pulpar, geminates occur mostly in word medial position. No geminate consonants occur in word final position. This constraint is due to the fact that Pulpar does not allow more than one consonant in word initial and final positions. Certain consonants can be geminated in word initial position as illustrated by the data in (3.3.3.1) and (3.3.3.2).

3.3.3.1	3.3.3.2
celal [celal]	cellal [ccellal]
pelal [pelal]	pellal [ppellal]
malal [malal]	mallól [mmallól]
maje [maje]	majjere [mmajjere]
padʼal [padʼal]	padʼdʼal [ppadʼdʼal]

ɓalal [ɓalal]   ɓalli [ɓɓalli]
caɗi [caɗi]   caɗti [ccatti]
biloowo [biloowo]   billoowo [bbilloowo]
bile [bile]   bille [bbille]
cakalo [cakalo]   cakkagol [ccakkagol]
came [came]   cammeeje [ccammeeje]

The stem initial consonant in (3.3.3.2) is pronounced as a geminate. The presence of a geminate medial consonant affects the stem initial consonant. That is, when there is a medial geminate consonant the hard form of the word initial consonant is pronounced as a geminate counterpart of the hard simple form. This being the case, gemination can occur in word initial position. This type of gemination can be observed with other consonants that can normally be geminated as well. The gemination of the medial consonant causes the stem initial consonant to become geminated. This assumption is reinforced by the fact that word initial segments that have already undergone the hardening process become geminated in the presence of a medial geminate as in (3.3.3.3)

3.3.3.3
    saɗ + i [saɗi]
    caɗ + i [caɗi]
    caɗ + ti [ccatti]

When preceded by vowels, the word initial geminates are also maintained as in (3.3.3.4)

3.3.3.4
O fii mo mallól
[o fii mo mmallól]
O naati e péllél ngél
[o naatee ppéllél ngél]
Wuro heewngo majjere
[wuro heewngo mmajjere]
O wuji e ɓalli
[o wujee ɓɓalli]

The only consonants that do not undergo this initial gemination are /y, w, f, s, h/. Interestingly enough these consonants do not have geminate forms in nominal complexes.

Also, vowels in word initial position are also affected by the same phenomenon even though the realization is not the same as illustrated in (3.3.3.5) and (3.3.3.6).

3.3.3.5	3.3.3.6
Simple form	*Geminated form*
aduna [aduna]	addude [ʔaddude]
asi [asi]	acci [ʔacci]
ela [ela]	ella [ʔella]
udumere [udumere]	uddugol [ʔuddugól
oto [oto]	óttude [ʔóttude]

In this particular case, a glottal stop is inserted at the beginning of the word as in (3.3.3.6).

Word Initial Gemination

Word initial geminates do not occur when a long vowel intervenes between the word initial consonant and the word medial geminates as in (3.3.3.7).

3.3.3.7			
mooɣ +	de	-->	[moojje] not *[mmoojje]
daaɣ +	de	-->	[daajje] not *[ddaajje]
waaɣ +	de	-->	[waajje] not *[wwaajje]

In (3.3.3.7), the initial consonant is not geminated when there is a long vowel intervening between the medial geminate and the word initial consonant.

When the word initial segment is a type that does not have a geminate counterpart, word initial gemination does not occur. The data in (3.3.3.8) illustrates this restriction.

3.3.3.8
    sakkaade
    hettere
    fittude
    rókkude

In (3.3.3.8) the word initial consonant is not geminated because it is not a consonant that is allowed to geminate. In addition, these consonants are not even changed into the forms that are allowed to geminate. So the analysis regarding consonant hardening will not apply in this particular case. But if the word initial consonant is already in its hard form the presence of the word medial geminate leads to the gemination of the word initial consonant.

A number of questions can arise regarding how to account for this word initial gemination and how to represent these geminates. Both questions are addressed in the following section.

The initial gemination process can not be analyzed in terms of assimilation even though the gemination of the word initial consonant is triggered by the presence of the medial geminate. Another alternative is to view this initial gemination in terms of weight. As shown in previous studies (Hayes 1989) a segment can acquire weight when it is in a weight position. So the presence of a medial geminate renders the word initial position a weight position to which two skeletal slots are assigned. This word initial gemination is captured by the rule in (3.3.3.9).

3.3.3.9

```
C  --->   C     /# - V  C
|        / \         / \
X      X   X       X   X
```

Conclusion

Various gemination processes were analyzed in this chapter. The analysis has also shown the inadequacy of previous analyses of gemination processes that obtain in Pulpar and a more general analysis was adopted that captures better the processes involved. The proposed analysis differs from those of Paradis (1986a, 1992) and Paradis and Prunet (1989) Bakovic (1995) in various ways. The differences relate to triggers for gemination, the types of consonants that have geminate counterparts, the status of the {in} suffix and their failure to analyze word initial gemination processes.

CHAPTER 4

METRICAL STRUCTURE CONSTRAINTS

Introduction

The identification of stress in Pulaar is usually done with reference mainly to pitch. The use of pitch as the means to identify stress is due to the fact that vowel length is phonemic in Pulaar. The adopted analysis provides a comprehensive analysis of the metrical structure of single words in isolation, words with derivational suffixes and sentences. In addition, the present analysis shows that previous analyses of Fula word stress assignment proposed by Taylor (1953), Arnott (1970), McIntosh (1984) and Prunet and Tellier (1984) are inadequate.

4.1 Relevant Literature

4.1.1 Taylor's Analysis

Taylor (1953) makes a few interesting remarks about the assignment of stress in Fula. He remarks that "the accent is predominantly a stress accent, and, generally speaking, depends on the long vowels".
He suggests the following rules for disyllables.
According to the first generalization, the accent falls on the first vowel if it is a long vowel or a diphthong. This observation is illustrated in the examples in (4.1.1.1).

> 4.1.1.1
> > suu'du
> > wee'ndu

The second generalization indicates that if the word has two consonants in the middle, or the first vowel is short, the accent is even. This pattern is exemplified in (4.1.1.2).

4.1.1.2

    nagge

    dimngal

In (4.1.1.3) the accent is on the last syllable.

    4.1.1.3

        O warai'

        noogaa's

In addition, for trisyllabic complexes, he suggests that the accent falls on the penultimate syllable with a long vowel. This generalization is illustrated in (4.1.1.4).

    4.1.1.4

        rawaa'ndu

Another generalization concerning trisyllabic complexes indicates that the accent falls on the first syllable if the vowel in the penultimate syllable is short. This generalization is illustrated in (4.1.1.5).

    4.1.1.5

        kaa'fa hi

Taylor makes an interesting generalization about polysyllables when he indicates that in such structures, the accent is free, but is usually on the penultimate, unless a long vowel attracts it to another syllable. This pattern is exemplified in (4.1.1.6).

    4.1.1.6

        ka'ɓ ɓan tee' ɗo

Taylor's remarks concerning the metrical system of Fula capture various generalizations. His attempt to divide the stress spectrum into disyllabic, trisyllabic and polysyllabic entities is very useful even though it misses important generalizations. His most important remark concerns his view of the predominance of syllables with long vowels over syllables containing short ones. This remark is very crucial even though he does not elaborate on it. In what follows, Taylor's generalizations are assessed.

    Taylor's first generalization is partially correct. For disyllables, the major stress falls on the first syllable of the word. The first generalization is partially incorrect because the placement of the major stress in disyllables does not depend on the length of the vowel of the first syllable.

The major stress is placed on the first syllable by default since the last syllable of the word is extrametrical. The extrametricality of the last syllable leaves only one "candidate" open for major stress assignment, the first syllable of the word. The second generalization concerning the accent being even if the word has two consonants in the middle is not plausible at all since a word cannot have more than one major stress. The third generalization is inaccurate. The last syllable never carries the major stress except in the case where a lexically stressed suffix occurs at the end of a word. The fourth generalization is partially correct because it works only if the penultimate syllable is the most sonorous syllable in the word as in (4.1.1.7).

4.1.1.7
"ra waa' ndu

The generalization makes a correct prediction concerning the placement of the major stress in this particular case. The generalization is incorrect when the penultimate syllable with a long vowel is preceded by a syllable which is more sonorous than or equally sonorous to the penultimate syllable. If the syllable preceding the penultimate syllable is equally sonorous to the penultimate syllable, the major stress falls by default on the former syllable as in (4.1.1.8).

4.1.1.8
mii' jii ɗo

Following Taylor's fourth generalization, the major stress will be assigned to the penultimate syllable since it has a long vowel. However, the major stress falls on the first syllable instead. If the syllable preceding the penultimate syllable is more sonorous than the penultimate syllable, the former bears the major stress as in (4.1.1.9).

4.1.1.9
baa'l dii ɗo

In (4.1.1.9), the major stress does not fall on the penultimate syllable even though it has a long vowel. Instead, it falls on the first syllable.

The fifth generalization is accurate and sound. In the absence of a heavy syllable, the major stress falls, by default, on the first syllable of the word.

Despite Taylor's generalizations, his treatment of the metrical system of Fula falls short in that it does not account for all stress patterns. Besides, there are many exceptions to his rules and observations. In his attempt to analyze the metrical structure of Fula, he does not view the last syllable of the word as extrametrical. The extrametricality of the last syllable is a crucial aspect in the analysis of the metrical system of Pulaar.

4.1.2 Arnott's Analysis

Arnott (1970) examines Fula stress patterns using a dialect of Fula called Gombe and he makes various generalizations. According to Arnott, the major stress is generally placed on the first syllable as this can be inferred from the statement: "The first syllable is the salient syllable."
For disyllabic nominals, he indicates that "...some have a salient first syllable, while in others the second syllable is salient."
He also remarks that "In interrogatives, the second syllable is salient..."
In his analysis of verbal complexes, he makes the following remark.

> As a general rule, the salient syllable of any verbal complex is the first syllable of the radical. But in complexes of the stative and continuous tenses and of the negative tenses, a different syllable is salient.

Arnott's general observation on stress assignment is that stress occurs on the first syllable of the word.
From these observations, it is clear that stress assignment is not accounted for in a principled and satisfactory manner. Following the generalization, one cannot in any way predict where the major stress is to be assigned. In addition, there exist many exceptions to Arnott's generalizations.

4.1.3 McIntosh's Analysis

McIntosh (1984) also deals with stress assignment in Fula using the Kaceccereere dialect. She recognizes the complexity of the stress system by her introductory sentence in which she remarks that "The identification of the stressed syllable in a word is not a simple matter."

Then she makes a generalization concerning word stress patterns in nominals.

> In nominals, it (stress) occurs on the last non final CVC or CVV syllable. In the absence of such a syllable, the initial syllable of the nominal is stressed, regardless of its structure.

The following data illustrate her generalizations concerning the assignment of the major stress.

naw li raa' wo
joo' ɗor ki

nja'w di ri
ka ce'c ce re ʔen

fa' ji ri
pa' ma ro

The analysis proposed by McIntosh is better structured and it accounts for many stress patterns that obtain in Pulaar. Her treatment of stress patterns in nominals without a heavy syllable is sound and correct. Her treatment of nominals with heavy penultimate syllables of the structure CVV or CVC captures certain generalizations but misses various other aspects. Actually, CVC and CVV syllables are not the only heavy syllables that occur in a penultimate position. Her treatment captures only instances where the penultimate syllable is the only heavy syllable in the word. However, in certain instances, both first and penultimate syllables are heavy. In these cases, the major stress is not always assigned to the penultimate syllable. Depending on the "sonority" hierarchy among the syllables involved, the major stress could be assigned either to the first or penultimate syllables. Her analysis does not mention four or five syllable words where CVVC, CVC, CVV and CV syllables are mixed in a word. Even though her analysis is a major improvement over Arnott and Taylor's analyses, it is not satisfactory.

4.1.4 Prunet and Tellier's Analysis

According to Prunet and Tellier (1984)

> ... the main stress falls on the first heavy syllable (CVV, CVC) starting from the left (beginning of the word). Other heavy syllables in the word will carry secondary stress. Light syllables do not carry stress. In the absence of a heavy syllable in a word, the first vowel carries the major stress.

They list a few examples showing the placement of the major and secondary stresses. Some of their examples are repeated in (4.1.4.1).

    4.1.4.1

        eɓe loo' to tir ki nan noo
        eɓe mba ro ndi'r ki nan noo
        eɓe nde wo ti rii'
        eɓe ko'l lo ndi rii

Prunet and Tellier's analysis is closely related to that of McIntosh. The same remarks made concerning the shortcomings of McIntosh's analysis are also applicable to Prunet and Tellier's account.

One important aspect of Prunet and Tellier's analysis that is particularly relevant to this study shows that CVV syllables are heavier than CVC syllables and consequently the former will carry the major stress over the latter.

Their analysis of the vowel shortening processes that obtain in Pulaar is useful despite numerous exceptions. They also indicate that " this alternation (long vs short) never affects a vowel in the first syllable of the root: any vowel in this position can be long or short".

The analysis of gemination processes and constraints shows that the vowel shortening rule can also apply to long vowels in syllable initial position.

Following the assessment of the analyses of Taylor, Arnott, McIntosh and Prunet and Tellier, focus is now directed to the analysis of Pulaar metrical structure.

4.2 Pulaar Metrical structure

Prior to providing an analysis, the stress patterns that obtain in the language are provided along with examples to illustrate these patterns.

4.2.1 Stress Patterns

Primary Stress
The data in (4.2.1.1) displays various stress patterns.

    4.2.1.1

        a'ba bo
        wu'de re
        a'l ku lal
        a'sa maan

Two observations can be made about the above data. First, the last syllable is never assigned the major stress whether it is light or heavy. Second, the major stress falls on the first syllable of the word. Additional data is considered in (4.2.1.2) to determine the adequacy of the above generalizations.

4.2.1.2
ji yaa' do
fo doo' re
ja maa' nu
bo na'n de

The data in (4.2.1.2) indicates that the second observation is inadequate since the stress does not fall on the first syllable of the word. Instead, it falls on the penultimate syllable. This second observation needs to be revised to account for the data presented so far. The major stress is placed on the heavy non-final syllable. In the absence of a heavy final syllable, the major stress is placed on the first syllable of the word. This observation accounts for the data presented so far. The adequacy of this revised observation is tested against additional data in (4.2.1.3).

4.2.1.3
ta'k kor di
maa' maa re
yaa' kaa re

As formulated, the revised observation does not account for the data in (4.2.1.3). In (4.2.1.3) two heavy non final syllables occur but the revised observation does not indicate which one bears the major stress. This observation is then revised to accommodate the set of data in (4.2.1.3). The major stress falls on the heavy non final syllable of the word if it is the only heavy non final syllable in the word. In the presence of two non final heavy syllables, the stress is placed on the first syllable of the word. In the absence of a heavy non final syllable, stress the first syllable of the word. This revision accounts for the data presented so far.

The adequacy of these revisions is tested against the data in (4.2.1.4).

4.2.1.4
hal kaa' de
fer laa' de
haf taa' de

The revisions cannot account for the placement of the major stress in (4.2.1.4). In fact, even though two heavy non final syllables occur in the words in (4.2.1.4), the major stress is not placed on the first syllable of the words as predicted by the latest revised proposal which will then require further revisions in terms of the structure of the non final heavy syllables. If the non final heavy syllables are of the CVC and CVV patterns, then the major stress falls on the syllable with a CVV structure. This revised proposal accounts for the cases in (4.2.1.4). In order to determine the suitability of this newly revised proposal, another set of data is considered in (4.2.1.5).

4.2.1.5

jaa taa'r naa jo
njaa yee'm naa jo
naa naa'l de

The newly revised proposal does not account for the data in (4.2.1.5) as it does not indicate the position of the major stress. In order to account for these problematic data, a revision of the latest proposal is required. This revision is done in terms of the structure of the syllables involved as this seems to be the determining factor for the assignment of the major stress. When non final heavy syllables have the structure CVV and CVVC, the major stress falls on the non final CVVC syllable. The adequacy of this revised proposal is tested against additional data in 4.2.1.6).

4.2.1.6

haa'l pu laar ʔen

The revised proposal does not indicate where to place the major stress in this particular case. In the presence of two non final heavy syllables of the structure CVVC, the proposal does not indicate where the major stress is to be placed. In order to account for these data, one needs to indicate that in the presence of heavy non final syllables of the structure CVVC, the major stress falls on the leftmost heavy syllable of the word.

The observations that have been made so far indicate that the placement of the major stress is determined by the weight of the heavy syllable.

In view of the above observations, the generalizations on Pulaar stress patterns are formulated in (4.2.1.7).

4.2.1.7

-The last syllable of the word is never stressed.
-Stress the first syllable if there is no heavy syllable in the word as in (4.2.1.7.1).

4.2.1.7.1
    a' du na
    a' la be

-Stress the penultimate syllable if it is the only heavy syllable in the word as in (4.2.1.7.2).

4.2.1.7.2
    ma laa ' ɗo
    da do'r de

-When both first and penultimate syllables have the same structure CVC, CVV or CVVC, stress the first syllable as in (4.2.1.7.3).

4.2.1.7.3
    ta'l lor de
    poo' laa ɗo
    haa'l pu laar ʔen

-When both first and penultimate syllables are heavy but with different weight, stress the heaviest syllable. CVVC is heavier than CVV which in turn is heavier than CVC which is heavier than CV. This generalization is illustrated in (4.2.1.7.4).

4.2.1.7.4
    hal kaa' de
    gaa's to too ɗo
    ha'l ku de

Secondary Stress

In their analysis of Pulaar metrical structure, while referring to secondary stress, Prunet and Tellier (1984) indicate that "The other heavy syllables of the word carry secondary stress." p.81

Even though they assert the presence of secondary stress in words, their rendering of the placement of the secondary stress is not accurate. Their claim for the placement of secondary stresses on every heavy syllable can lead to stress clash as illustrated in (4.2.1.8).

4.2.1.8
    j`aa taa'r n`aa jo

In (4.2.1.8), the syllable carrying the major stress is immediately preceded and followed by heavy syllables to which their analysis will assign secondary stresses thus leading to stress clash.

In addition, stress systems tend to show some alternation between stressed and unstressed syllables. In Prunet and Tellier's analysis, this alternation between stressed and unstressed syllables will not obtain in instances of the type illustrated in (4.2.1.8). Secondary stress occurs only in nominal and verbal complexes of four or more syllables. In disyllabic complexes, the last syllable is extrametrical and the major stress falls on the first syllable of the word. Therefore, secondary stress cannot occur in disyllabic complexes. In trisyllabic words, the last syllable is also always extrametrical. The major stress can occur either on the first or second syllable of the word. Even though this might leave the syllable that does not carry the major stress open for secondary stress assignment, the unstressed syllable will not carry secondary stress because there must be an intervening syllable between the syllable carrying the major stress and the one carrying the secondary stress. This type of situation never arises in trisyllabic complexes. For these reasons trisyllabic complexes do not carry secondary stress.

Only heavy syllables can carry a secondary stress. A heavy syllable that is adjacent to the syllable carrying the major stress does not carry secondary stress. A secondary stress can occur in any position except in syllable final position.

The data in (4.2.1.9) illustrates the presence of secondary stress in tetrasyllabic and pentasyllabic complexes.

        4.2.1.9

                j`ol ti noo' wo
                baa' bal n`aa jo
                haa'l pu l`aar ʔen
                ɗaa' no to n`oo ɗo
                k`aa sa maa's naa jo
                gaa's to to n`oo ɗo

The occurrence of secondary stress can be prevented by two destressing (stress deletion) rules, rule 1 and rule 2.

    Rule 1   *Rule 2*

```
*        *          *    *
*  *     *          *  *     *
*  * --> *  *        *  * --> *  *
V  V     V V         V  V     V  V
```

The operation of these destressing rules is shown in due course. Following the discussion of the facts concerning the assignment of stress, the subsequent section focuses on the type of analysis that Halle and Vergnaud's approach may provide for the analysis of Pulaar metrical structure.

4.3 ANALYSIS

The following analysis may be the type that can be provided within the Halle and Vergnaud's framework to account for Pulaar metrical structure.

4.3.1 Halle and Vergnaud's Analysis

Vowels that are heads are stress bearing elements
The last syllable is extrametrical
-Assign an asterisk to every syllable
-Assign another asterisk to a syllable with a long vowel
-Assign another asterisk to a closed syllable
Line 0 parameter settings are [+HT, -BND, right to left and left].
Construct constituents on line 0 and project the head(s) on line 1.
Line 1 parameter settings are [+HT, -BND, right to left and left].
Construct constituents on line 1 and project the head(s) on line 2.

In order to determine the adequacy of this analysis, it is tested against the data in (4.3.11).

    4.3.1.1

       ba'la be
       (* *)<*>   0
       *   1

The data in (4.3.1.1) is accounted for by the proposed analysis. Additional data is provided in (4.3.1.2) to further test the proposed analysis.

    4.3.1.2

       ta'l lor de
       * * <*>   0
       (* *)   1
       *   2

baa'waa ɗo
```
*   *   <*>      0
(*   *)           1
    *            2
```

The last syllables are extrametrical. By virtue of being closed or long syllables, these are assigned a line 1 grid mark. Constructing constituents on line 1 and projecting the heads will provide the correct output. However, secondary stresses occur where they are not expected. In order to eliminate these secondary stresses, the first destressing rule is applied. The proposed analysis works for the data presented so far. The adequacy of the analysis is tested against additional data in (4.3.1.3).

4.3.1.3

ji yaa' ɗo
```
(* *) <*>      0
*   *          1
```

In (4.3.1.3), two asterisks appear on line 0 one of which is the head of the constituent constructed from line 0 and the other asterisk which was already present on line 1. Constructing a left headed constituent on line 1 and projecting the head on line 2 leads to the derivation of the structure in (4.3.1.4).

4.3.1.4

ji yaa' ɗo
```
(* *) <*>      0
(* *)          1
*              2
```

This, however, is not the correct output. As a matter of fact, the major stress ends on the first syllable instead of the second syllable. The derivation of the correct output necessitates a stress shift rule which shifts the stress to its correct position. Following Davis (1988), this stress shift rule is formulated in (4.3.1.5).

4.3.1.5

Stress Shift Rule

Shift a line 2 grid mark from the first to the second syllable if the second syllable is heavy and the first syllable is light.

The application of this stress shift rule will lead to the output in (4.3.1.6).

    4.3.1.6

        ji yaa' ɗo
        (* *) <*>   0
        (* *)   1
          *   2

A secondary stress appears incorrectly on the first syllable. In order to eliminate this secondary stress, the second destressing rule is applied and the correct output is derived in (4.3.1.7).

    4.3.1.7

        ji yaa' ɗo
        (* *) <*>   0
          *   1
          *   2

The adequacy of the proposed analysis is assessed against additional data in (4.3.1.8).

    4.3.1.8

        jaa taa'r naa jo
         *   *   * <*> 0
         *   *   *   1
            *   2

Constructing one constituent on line 1 and projecting the head on line 2 yields the output in (4.3.1.9).

    4.3.1.9

        jaa taa'r naa jo
         *   *   * <*> 0
        (*   *   *)   1
         *   *   2

Constructing a constituent on line 2 and projecting the head on line 3 and conflating lines 1 and 2 (erasing line 1) yields the structure in (4.3.1.10).

4.3.1.10

In order to account for this type of data, a revision of the stress shift rule is required. The revision of the stress shift rule is formulated in the following.

Shift a line 2 grid mark from the first to the second syllable if the second syllable is heavier than the first. The application of this revised stress shift rule to the structure in (4.3.1.10) results in the following structure.

```
jaa taa'r naa jo
*    *    * <*>    0
(*    *)          1
     *           2
```

However, an incorrectly placed secondary stress occurs in the first syllable. The second destressing rule applies, eliminating the secondary stress and the correct output is derived in (4.3.1.11).

4.3.1.11

```
jaa taa'r naa jo
*    *    * <*>    0
     *           1
     *           2
```

The proposed analysis appears to account for the data presented thus far. In order to determine the adequacy of this analysis, it is tested against additional data in (4.3.1.12).

4.3.1.12

```
jol ti noo' wo
*   *   *   <*>    0
(*        *)       1
 *                2
```

The proposed analysis leads to the incorrect placement of the major stress on the first syllable. Applying the stress shift rule shifts the stress to its normal position.

The proposed analysis appears to provide an account of the metrical structure of Pulaar. On a number of instances, the need to refer to the weight of the syllable in order to derive the correct output arises. The assignment of the major stress is determined by the weight of the syllables in the string. Consequently, an analysis of Pulaar metrical structure is proposed that is based on the weight hierarchy among the syllables in the language.

4.3.2 Proposed Analysis

The analysis proposed here to capture word stress assignment in Pulaar is described in the following.

1a) Stress bearing elements are vowels

1b) Vowels that are head of rhymes are stress bearing

2) The last syllable of the word is marked extrametrical

3) Line 0 parameter settings are [+HT, +BND, right to left]

On line 0, construct binary left headed constituents if the left syllable in the constituent is equal to or more sonorous than the right syllable; otherwise, construct right headed constituents.

Project the head(s) on line 1

4) Line 1 parameters are [+HT, +BND, right to left].

On line 1, construct binary left headed constituents if the left syllable in the constituent is equal to or more sonorous than the right syllable; otherwise construct right headed constituents.

Project the head(s) on line 2

5) Line 2 parameter settings are [+HT, +BND, right to left]

If necessary, on line 2, construct binary left headed constituents if the left syllable in the constituent is equal to or more sonorous than the right syllable in the constituent; otherwise construct right-headed constituents.

Project the head on line 3

6) Apply the appropriate stress deletion rule(s) 1 and / or 2 to eliminate the incorrect placement of the secondary stress

In Pulaar and other dialects of Fula, the occurrence of long vowels is very common. The long vowel is represented by the duplication of the vowel phoneme as illustrated in the inventory of the segments and syllables. The first vowel of the vowel sequence is the head of the rhyme.

The analysis adopted not only makes use of the extrametricality concept but also shows the importance of this feature in the analysis of Pulaar metrical structure. The last syllable of the string is always extrametrical. The extrametricality of the last syllable was hinted at by McIntosh when she indicated that "In nominals, it (stress) occurs on the last non final CVC or CVV syllable." The extrametricality of the last syllable is a crucial aspect in the analysis of the metrical system of Pulaar. The extrametricality of the last syllable explains why the major stress does not fall on the last syllable in (4.3.2.1).

    4.3.2.1

       noo' gaas
       de'b buus

In (4.3.2.1) the last syllable is more sonorous than the first syllable. It is then expected to attract the major stress but it does not. The last syllable does not attract the major stress because it is extrametrical.

The above analysis is applied to all types of word combinations that obtain in Pulaar. For the sake of convenience and ease of exposition, the presentation is segmented into sections dealing with nominals and verbal complexes, single words in isolation and words with derivational affixes and sentences.

Nominal Complexes

The stress patterns of single words are discussed with reference to nominal complexes. The operation of the proposed analysis is shown by means of derivations which are supplemented by a discussion of the relevant aspects.

The placement of the major stress is indicated by (') following the stressed vowel. The placement of the secondary stress is indicated by (`) before the vowel that carries this secondary stress.

4.3.3.1 Monosyllabic Nominals

In monosyllabic nominal complexes, as expected, the major stress occurs on the only syllable of the word. The data in (4.3.3.1.1).

    4.3.3.1.1

       mool
       paas
       jom
       (*)   0
        *   1

4.3.3.2 Disyllabic Nominals

In nominals of two syllables, the major stress falls by default on the first syllable of the word regardless of its structure as in (4.3.3.2.1).
4.3.3.2.1
    ba'y lo
    (*) <*> 0
    *   1

    lo'r so
    (*) <*> 0
    *   1

    joo'w re
    (*) <*>   0
    *   1

    ɓa' lal
    (*)<*> 0
    *   1

    pu' laar
    (* <*> 0
    *   1

The data in (4.3.3.2.1) confirms Arnott's observation according to which the first syllable is assigned the major stress. In other words, the major stress falls, by default, on the first syllable since the last syllable is extrametrical. The postulation of the extrametricality of the last syllable can be observed in the last two instances in which the last syllable is heavy but never carries stress. Also, the assignment of the major stress to the first syllable of the word follows from the proposed analysis. That is, since the last syllable is always extrametrical, it does not carry the major stress which falls on the only remaining syllable in the disyllabic words.

4.3.3.3 Trisyllabic Nominals

In single trisyllabic nominals, the assignment of the major stress is highly determined by the structure of the first and penultimate syllables since the last syllable is always extrametrical. Therefore, all possible patterns for first and penultimate syllables are examined. The first pattern is the combination of a first light syllable with heavy penultimate syllables. The structure of the last syllable is not important since that syllable is extrametrical. Possible combinations of this type of data are illustrated in (4.3.3.3.1).

4.3.3.3.1
fi ji'r de
ɓa taa' ke
(* *) <*>   0
*   1

In (4.3.3.3.1), the major stress is placed on the penultimate syllable, the only heavy syllable in the word. Applying the analysis, a binary right-headed constituent is constructed since the left syllable in the constituent is less sonorous than the right syllable. The head is then projected on line 1.

Another pattern is the combination of first heavy syllables and a light penultimate syllable. The possible combinations of this sort are illustrated in (4.3.3.3.2).

4.3.3.3.2
ta'l ku ru
pii' la gol
(* *)<*>   0
*   1

In (4.3.3.3.2), the major stress is assigned to the first syllable of the word. On line 0 the last syllable is marked extrametrical and a left headed constituent is constructed since the left syllable in the constituent is more sonorous than the right one. The head is then projected on line 1.

Another pattern (CV'C CVC CV) is obtained when both first and penultimate syllables are of the CVC type as in (4.3.3.3.3).

4.3.3.3.3
ta'l lor de
go'l lor de
(* *)<*>   0
*   1

In this case, both first and penultimate syllables are of CVC types. The major stress is assigned to the first syllable of the word. Applying the analysis, a binary left headed constituent is constructed since the left syllable in the constituent is equally sonorous to the right syllable. The head is then projected on line 1.

Another pattern (CVV' CVV CV) that obtains in the language is when both first and penultimate syllables are of the CV type as in (4.3.3.3.4).

    4.3.3.3.4
        baa' waa ɗo
        naa' too wo
        (* *) <*>   0
        *   1

In (4.3.3.3.4) the major stress falls on the first syllable of the word even though the first and penultimate syllables are of the CV type.

So far, the major stress is placed on the heavy penultimate if the first syllable of the word is light. If the first syllable is heavy, it carries major stress.

In what follows, different types of heavy syllables are combined to show the operation of the proposed analysis. An example of this type of data is provided in (4.3.3.3.5).

    4.3.3.3.5
        gay naa' ko
        jal too' wo
        (* *) <*>   0
        *   1

The data in (4.3.3.3.5) confirms the analysis of McIntosh according to which the major stress is generally placed on the penultimate syllable which has the CVC or CV structures. As observed, the major stress is placed on the penultimate syllable, not on the first syllable of the word. On line 0 the last syllable is marked extrametrical and a right headed constituent is constructed since the right syllable in the constituent is more sonorous than the left syllable. The head is then projected on line 1 and the correct output is derived.

However, as indicated earlier, there are exceptions to McIntosh's analysis. Indeed, in (4.3.3.3.4) and (4.3.3.3.5), the major stress does not fall on the penultimate syllable even though it is a heavy syllable. Actually, the major stress falls on the first syllable of the word.

In addition to these trisyllabic nominals, other trisyllabic nominals exist which do not have a heavy syllable either in penultimate or first syllable positions. In these trisyllabic nominals, the primary stress falls by default on the first syllable of the word as in (4.3.3.3.6).

4.3.3.3.6

    a' du na
    ba' la be
    ko' la ngal
    (* *) <*>   0
    *   1

Applying the analysis, the last syllable is made extrametrical. A binary left headed constituent is constructed since the left syllable in the constituent is equally sonorous to the right syllable in the constituent. The head is projected on line 1.

In addition to the above, the analysis is applied to three syllable words of the structure CVV CVVC ?VC in (4.3.3.3.7).

4.3.3.3.7

    jaa suu's ?en
    (* *) <*>   0
    *   1

Here again, the last syllable is extrametrical. On line 0 a binary right headed constituent is constructed since the left syllable in the constituent is less sonorous than the right syllable in the constituent. The head is then projected on line 1.

Another type of three syllable word categories is exemplified in (4.3.3.3.8).

4.3.3.3.8

    naa naa'l de
    maa maa'y de
    guu huu'n ɗe
    (*   *)   <*> 0
    *   1

In (4.3.3.3.7) and (4.3.3.3.8), the major stress falls on the CVVC syllable, the heaviest syllable in the string. This situation obtains only because the CVVC syllable is heavier than the CV syllable. If the consonant in the coda position does not contribute to the weight of the syllable, then the major stress would not fall on the CVVC syllable.

4.3.3.4 Tetrasyllabic Nominals

The stress patterns of four syllable words is fairly consistent. The major stress usually falls on the first or penultimate syllables of the word. One type of pattern (C`VC CV CVV' CV) is illustrated in (4.3.3.4.1).

4.3.3.4.1

```
        j`oϒ ϒi noo' wo
        b`al  li  noo' wo
        (*) (*  *)  <*> 0
        (*      *)       1
                *         2
```

In (4.3.3.4.1), both first and penultimate syllables are heavy. The major stress is placed on the penultimate syllable which is more sonorous than the first syllable. As expected, the first syllable of the words in (4.3.3.4.1) carries a secondary stress. Another type of tetrasyllabic nominals is illustrated in (4.3.3.4.2).

4.3.3.4.2
```
    jaa' fo t`oo ɗo
    taa' ni r`aa ɗo
    baa' hi r`aa ɗo
    (*) (*  *) <*> 0
    (*      *)      1
            *        2
```

As predicted by the analysis, the major stress falls on the first syllable of the word when both first and penultimate syllables have equal sonority. Both syllables have CV patterns. On line 0 a binary right headed constituent is constructed since the left syllable in the constituent is less sonorous than the right syllable. On line 1 a binary left headed constituent is constructed since both syllables in the constituent have equal sonority. The head is then projected on line 2. The penultimate syllables in (4.3.3.4.2) carry the secondary stress as expected.

Another type of four syllable words is exemplified in (4.3.3.4.3).

4.3.3.4.3
```
        ja mi roo' wo
        jo go too' ɗo
        (*)(*  *) <*>        0
        (*     *)            1
               *             2
```

Unlike other four syllable words, only one heavy syllable occurs in this word. Following the predictions of the analysis proposed here, the major stress is placed on the heaviest syllable of the word. On line 0 the last syllable is marked extrametrical and two constituents are constructed the first of which is a degenerate foot and the second a binary constituent. On line 1 a right headed constituent is constructed and the head is projected on line 2. The correct output is derived as far as the placement of the major stress is concerned. However, an incorrect secondary stress occurs. The application of stress deletion rule 2 deletes the secondary stress and the correct output is derived as in (4.3.3.4.4).

4.3.3.4.4

```
        du wa naa do
        (*) (*   *) <*>   0
                  *        1
                  *        2
```

In addition to the above four syllable word patterns, another different structure is illustrated in (4.3.3.4.5).

4.3.3.4.5

```
        baa'l di ge lam
        kaa'l di ge lam
        (*)  (*  *)<*>   0
        (*   *)          1
         *               2
```

Again, the major stress is assigned to the heaviest syllable of the word as predicted by the analysis. These constituents are left-headed following the principles of the analysis. However, a secondary stress appears in a position where it is not expected to occur. The application of the first stress deletion rule 1 eliminates the incorrectly placed secondary stress and the correct output is derived in (4.3.3.4.6).

4.3.3.4.6

```
        kaa'l di ge lam
        (*)  (*  *)<*>   0
         *               1
         *               2
```

In order to determine the adequacy of the analysis, it is tested against other types of tetrasyllabic structures. The next type of structure (CVV'C CVC CV CVC) is illustrated in (4.3.3.4.7).

4.3.3.4.7

    poo'f tor ge   lam
    maa'n tor ge lam
    (*) (*   *)<*>   0
    (*   *)   1
     *   2

The major stress falls, as predicted by the analysis, on the heaviest and more sonorous syllable of the word. The secondary stress on the second syllable is eliminated by the application of the first stress deletion rule and the correct output is derived in (4.3.3.4.8).

4.3.3.4.8

    gaa's tir ge lam
    maa'n tor ge lam
    (*) (* *)<*> 0
    *   1
    *   2

Another type of tetrasyllabic nominal structure (CVV'C CV C`VVC CVC) is illustrated in (4.3.3.4.9).

4.3.3.4.9

    haa'l pu l`aar ?en
    (*)   (* *) <*>   0
    (*   *)   1
    *   2

The data in (4.3.3.4.9) is also different from all previous types of data listed under four syllable words. In (4.3.3.4.9), CVVC syllable structures occur in both first and penultimate positions. Again, the major stress falls on the first syllable of the word as predicted by the analysis. The secondary stress also occurs where predicted.

Another type of four syllable words has the structure ^{n}CVV CVVC CV CV. This tetrasyllabic structure is illustrated in (4.3.3.4.10).

4.3.3.4.10

    jaa taa'r naa jo
    ^{n}jaa yee'm naa jo
    ^{n}jaa ree'm naa jo
    (*)(*   *)<*>   0
    (* *)   1
    *   2

In (4.3.3.4.10), the major stress falls on the antepenult, the most sonorous syllable in the word. The proposed analysis correctly predicts where the major stress occurs. On line 0 a bounded binary constituent is constructed from right to left and a degenerate foot is constructed for the first syllable of the word. The binary constituent is left headed since the left syllable in the constituent is more sonorous than the right syllable. The heads are projected on line 1 where a bounded constituent is constructed, right to left. Since the right syllable in the constituent is more sonorous than the left syllable, the foot is right headed. The head is projected on line 2. The application of stress deletion rule 2 eliminates the incorrectly placed secondary stress on the first syllable of the string.

The application of the proposed analysis to two, three, four syllable nominals has not been problematic in any of the instances discussed. The same analysis is tested against pentasyllabic nominals.

4.3.3.5 Pentasyllabic Nominals

The proposed analysis is applied to different combinations of five syllable words that obtain in the language. The data in (4.3.3.5.1) exemplifies one type of pentasyllabic complexes.

> 4.3.3.5.1
>> jo go to noo' ɗo
>> du wa na noo' ɗo
>> pi ya na noo' ɗo
>> (* *)(* *) <*>   0
>> (*   *)   1
>>   *   2

The application of the proposed analysis yields the correct output. On line 0, the constituent containing light syllables is left headed while the constituent containing the heavy syllable is right headed. Both heads are projected on line 1. The constituent on line 1 is right headed since the right syllable in the constituent is more sonorous than the left syllable. As predicted by the analysis, the major stress is placed on the penultimate syllable, the heaviest syllable in the word. A secondary stress occurs on the first syllable. Here again, applying stress deletion rule 2 removes this secondary stress and the correct output is derived in (4.3.3.5.2).

4.3.3.5.2
    le lo to noo' ɗo
    jo go to noo' ɗo
    (* *)(* *) <*>   0
        *   1
        *   2

Another type of pentasyllabic structure is illustrated in (4.3.3.5.3).
    4.3.3.5.3
        ɗaa' no to n`oo ɗo
        baa' lo to n`oo ɗo
        (*   *)(*   *) <*>   0
        (*   *)   1
         *   2

On line 0 the last syllable is marked extrametrical. Two binary
constituents are constructed. The one to the right is right headed and the
one to the left is left headed. The heads are projected on line 1 where a
binary left headed constituent is constructed whose head is projected on
line 2. As predicted by the analysis, the major stress falls on the first
syllable of the word. The secondary stress is also placed where it is
expected to occur.

Additional types of five syllable word structures (CVV CV CVVC CV
CV, CV CV CVVC CVV CV) are exemplified in (4.3.3.5.4) and
(4.3.3.5.5).
    4.3.3.5.4
        k`aa sa maa's naa jo
        (*   *) (*   *) <*>   0
        (*   *)   1
            *   2

    4.3.3.5.5
        su wee raa't naa jo
        nu waa soo'r naa jo
        (*   *) (*   *) <*>   0
         (*   *)   1
           *   2

In both (4.3.3.5.4) and (4.3.3.5.5) the heaviest syllable is preceded and followed by syllables of the CV patterns. However, the major stress falls on the CVVC syllable in antepenult position. The prominence of the CVVC syllable over the CV syllables causes the major stress to occur on the most prominent syllable. Here again, bounded binary constituents are constructed from right to left. Both heads are projected onto line 1 where a right headed bounded binary constituent is constructed since the right syllable in the constituent is more sonorous than the left syllable. The head is then projected on line 2. The predictions of the analysis are correctly realized. The application of stress deletion rule 2 eliminates the secondary stress in (4.3.3.5.5) and the correct output is derived in (4.3.3.5.6).

4.3.3.5.6

```
su wee raa't naa  jo
nu waa soo'r naa  jo
(*   *) (*    *) <*>      0
     (*  *)              1
        *               2
```

The data in (4.3.3.5.7) exemplify a CVV'C CV CV CVV CV pentasyllabic pattern.

4.3.3.5.7

```
laal to to noo ɗo
baal de te noo ɗo
(*    *)(*  *) <*>       0
(*          *)          1
*                      2
```

The last syllable is marked extrametrical and two binary feet are constructed. The one to the right is right headed as the syllable on the right is more sonorous than the one on the left. The left foot is left headed as the syllable on the left is more sonorous than the one to the right. Both heads are then projected onto line 1 where a binary left headed constituent is constructed. The head is then projected on line 2. As expected, a secondary stress occurs on the CVV syllable.

Another type of pentasyllabic structure (CVC CVC CV CVV' CV) is
illustrated in (4.3.3.5.8).

4.3.3.5.8
dar tin tu noo ɗo
pel lir tu noo ɗo
(* *) (* *) <*>   0
(*   *)   1
         *   2

In (4.3.3.5.8) the last syllable is marked extrametrical. Two binary feet are
constructed. The one to the right is right headed and the one to the left is
left headed. The heads are projected onto line 1 where a binary right
headed syllable is constructed. The head is then projected on line 2.
Another type of pentasyllabic structure (CV CVC CV CVV' CV) is
illustrated in (4.3.3.5.9).

4.3.3.5.9
de fir tu noo ɗo
ke lir tu noo ɗo
(* *) (* *) <*>   0
(*   *)   1
         *   2

In (4.3.3.5.9), the last syllable is marked extrametrical and two binary
right headed constituents are constructed. The heads are projected onto
line 1 where a binary right headed constituent is constructed. The head is
then projected on line 2. As expected, a secondary stress occurs on the
CVC syllable.
The next type of pentasyllabic nominal (CV' CV CV CV nCVC) is
illustrated in (4.3.3.5.10).

4.3.3.5.10
bo na ki ta ngel
la mo la mo ngal
(*   *)(*   *) <*>   0
(*   *)   1
         *   2

In (4.3.3.5.10) the last syllable is marked extrametrical on line 0 where
two binary left headed syllables are constructed. The heads are then
projected on line 1 where a left headed constituent is constructed whose
head is then projected on line 2. The application of stress deletion rule 1

eliminates the incorrect secondary stress.
The next pentasyllabic structure (CV CV CVC CVV' CV) is illustrated
in (4.3.3.5.11).

> 4.3.3.5.11
>
> ja mi ran noo ɗo
> (* *)(* *) <*>   0
> (*   *)   1
>   *   2

In (4.3.3.5.11) the last syllable is marked extrametrical and two binary
constituents are constructed. The one to the right is right headed and the
one to the left is left headed. The heads are projected on line 1 where a
binary right headed constituent is constructed whose head is then
projected on line 2. The incorrectly placed secondary stress is eliminated
by the application of the second stress deletion rule.
The next type of pentasyllabic structure (CVV' CVC CV CVV CV) is
exemplified in (4.3.3.5.12).

> 4.3.3.5.12
>
> ɗaa noy to noo ɗo
> baa joy to noo ɗo
> baa tir tu noo ɗo
> (* *)(* *) <*>   0
> (*   *)   1
> *   2

In (4.3.3.5.12) the last syllable is marked extrametrical on line 0 where
two binary constituents are constructed. The one to the right is right
headed and the one to the left is left headed. The heads are then projected
onto line 1 where a binary left headed constituent is formed whose head
is then projected on line 2. As expected, a secondary stress occurs on the
second CVV syllable.
The next pentasyllabic structure (CVC CVV' CV CV CVC)
is illustrated in (4.3.3.5.13)

> 4.3.3.5.13
>
> ham maa ya ro yel
> (*   *) (* *)<*>   0
>   (* *)   1
>   *   2

In (4.3.3.5.13) the last syllable is marked extrametrical on line 0 where two binary constituents are constructed. The one to the right is left headed while the one to the left is right headed. The heads are projected on line 1 where a binary left headed constituent is constructed whose head is then projected on line 2. The application of stress deletion rule 1 eliminates the incorrectly placed secondary stress.

The next type of pentasyllabic structure (CV CV nCVV CV) is exemplified in (4.3.3.5.14).

4.3.3.5.14
```
fa wo ndi roo 6e
wa ro ndi roo 6e
(*  *) (*  *) <*>        0
(*           *)          1
             *           2
```

In (4.3.3.5.14) the last syllable is marked extrametrical on line 0 where two binary constituents are constructed. The one to the right is right headed while the one to the left is left headed. The heads are projected onto line 1 where a binary right headed constituent is constructed whose head is then projected on line 2. The application of the second stress deletion rule eliminates the incorrectly placed secondary stress.

The next pentasyllabic nominal structure (CVC CV CVC CVV' CV) is exemplified in (4.3.3.5.15).

4.3.3.5.15
```
bal li nan noo do
god di nan noo do
(*  *)(*  *) <*>        0
(*          *)          1
            *           2
```

In (4.3.3.5.15), the last syllable is marked extra metrical on line 0 and two constituents are constructed. The one to the right is right headed and the one to the left is left headed. The heads of both constituents are projected on line 1 where a binary right headed constituent is constructed whose head is then projected on line 2. As expected, a secondary stress occurs on the first syllable.

The next pentasyllabic nominal complex structure (CV CV CV CVV' CV) is illustrated in (4.3.3.5.16).

    4.3.3.5.16

        le lo to noo ɗo
        da ro to noo ɗo
        (* *)(* *) <*>   0
        (*   *)   1
            *   2

In (4.3.3.5.16), the last syllable is marked extra metrical on line 0 where two binary constituents are constructed. The one to the right is right headed and the one to the left is left headed. Both heads are projected on line 1 where a binary right headed constituent is constructed whose head is projected on line 2. Contrary to expectation, a secondary stress occurs on the first syllable. The application of the second stress deletion rule eliminates the incorrectly placed secondary stress.

The next pentasyllabic structure (CVC CV CV CVV' CV) is exemplified in (4.3.3.5.17).

    4.3.3.5.17

        lel to to noo ɗo
        (* *)(* *) <*>   0
        (*   *)   1
            *   2

In (4.3.3.5.17) the last syllable in the string is marked extra metrical on line 0 where two binary constituents are constructed. The one to the right is right headed and the one to the left is left headed. The heads are projected on line 1 where a binary right headed constituent is constructed whose head is projected on line 2. As expected, a secondary stress occurs on the first syllable.

The next pentasyllabic nominal complex structure (CVV'C CVV CV CVV CV) is exemplified in (4.3.3.5.18).

    4.3.3.5.18

        naat naat ti noo wo
        (* *) (* *) <*> 0
        (*   *)   1
        *   2

In (4.3.3.5.18), the last syllable is marked extrametrical on line 0 where two binary constituents are constructed. The one to the right is right headed while the one to the left is left headed. The heads are projected on line 1 where a binary left headed constituent is constructed whose head is projected on line 2. As expected, a secondary stress occurs on the penultimate syllable.

The next pentasyllabic nominal complex structure (V CV CV CVV' CV) is exemplified in (4.3.3.5.19).

4.3.3.5.19

```
         i to  to noo ɗo
        (* *)(*  *) <*>   0
        (*       *)        1
              *            2
```

In (4.3.3.5.19) the last syllable is marked extrametrical on line 0 where two binary constituents are constructed. The heads are projected on line 1 where a binary right headed constituent is constructed whose head is projected on line 2. The application of the second stress deletion rule eliminates the incorrectly placed secondary stress on the first syllable.

The next pentasyllabic nominal complex structure (VV'C CVC CV CVV CV) is exemplified in (4.3.3.5.20).

4.3.3.5.20

```
         iir toy tu noo ɗo
        (* *) (*  *) <*>      0
        (*         *)          1
              *               2
```

In (4.3.3.5.20) the last syllable is marked extrametrical on line 0 where two binary constituents are constructed. The one to the right is right headed and the one to the left is left headed. The heads are projected on line 1 where a binary left headed constituent is constructed whose head is projected on line 2. As expected, a secondary stress occurs on the penultimate syllable.

The next pentasyllabic nominal complex structure (CVV'C CVV CV nCV CVC) is exemplified in (4.3.3.5.21).

4.3.3.5.21

```
         naat naa to ndi  ral
        (*    *) (*   *)<*>    0
        (*         *)          1
              *               2
```

In (4.3.3.5.21) the last syllable is marked extrametrical on line 0 where two binary left headed constituents are constructed whose heads are projected on line 1 where a binary left headed constituent is constructed whose head is projected on line 2. The application of the first stress deletion rule eliminates the incorrectly placed secondary stress on the third syllable.

The next pentasyllabic nominal complex structure (V CVC CV CVV' CV) is exemplified in (4.3.3.5.22).

4.3.3.5.22

```
        a moy tu noo ɓe
      (*   *) (*   *) <*>        0
         (*      *)              1
              *                  2
```

In (4.3.4.5.22), the last syllable is marked extrametrical on line 0 where two binary cosntituents are constructed. The heads are projected on line 1 where a binary right headed constituent is constructed whose head is projected on line 2. As expected, a secondary stress occurs on the second syllable.

The discussion in the previous section focused on pentasyllabic complexes of various structures. All structures were accounted for by the proposed analysis whose adequacy is tested against sextasyllabic structures.

4.3.3.6 Sextasyllabic Nominals

The first sextasyllabic structure is exemplified in (4.3.3.6.1).

4.3.3.6.1

```
        ca bo bi nan noo ɗo
      (*)(*   *)(*   *) <*>       0
      (*)(*        *)             1
      (*            *)            2
              *                   3
```

In (4.3.3.6.1), the last syllable is marked extra metrical on line 0 where two binary feet and one degenerate foot are constructed. The constituent to the right is right headed while the one to the left is left headed. The heads are projected on line 1 where a binary right headed constituent and a degenerate foot are constructed. The heads are projected on line 2 where a binary right headed constituent is constructed whose head is projected on line 3. The incorrectly place secondary stress on the first syllable is eliminated by the second stress deletion rule.

The next sextasyllabic structure (CVC CV CVC CV CVV' CV) is exemplified in (4.3.3.6.2).

    4.3.3.6.2

        bal li noy tu noo ɗo
        gar ti roy tu noo ɗo

(*) (* *) (* *) <*>		0
(*) (* *)		1
(* *)		2
*		3

In (4.3.3.6.2) the last syllable of the string is marked extra metrical on line 0 where two binary feet and one degenerate foot are constructed. The heads are then projected on line 1 where a binary constituent and a degenerate foot are constructed. The heads are then projected on line 2 where a binary right headed constituent is constructed whose head is then projected on line 3. Conflating lines 2 and 3 results in the following structure.

        bal li noy tu noo ɗo
        gar ti roy tu noo ɗo

(*) (* *) (* *) <*>		0
(*) (* *)		1
*		2

As expected, a secondary stress occurs on the first and third syllables.

The next sextasyllabic structure (CV CV CVC CV CVV' CV) is illustrated in (4.3.3.6.3).

    4.3.3.6.3

        ja mi roy tu noo ɗo

(*)(* *) (* *) <*>		0
(*) (* *)		1
(* *)		2
*		3

In (4.3.3.6.3), the last syllable is marked extra metrical on line 0 where two binary feet and one degenerate foot are constructed whose heads are then projected onto line 1. On line 1, one binary right headed constituent and one degenerate foot are constructed whose heads are projected onto line 2 where a binary right headed constituent is constructed whose head is projected on line 3. Conflating lines 2 and 3 results in the following structure.

```
ja mi roy tu noo ɗo
(*)(*  *) (*  *) <*>      0
(*)  (*    *)            1
     *                  2
```

The application of a stress deletion rule eliminates the incorrectly placed secondary stress on the light syllable at the beginning of the word. The next sextasyllabic structure (CVV'C CV CV CV CVV CV) is exemplified in (4.3.3.6.4).

    4.3.3.6.4

```
kaaŋ ɗi ki  no yii ɗo
(*)    (* *)(*  *) <*>      0
(*)   (*       *)          1
(*             *)          2
*                         3
```

In (4.3.3.6.4), the last syllable is marked extra metrical on line 0 where two binary constituents and one degenerate foot are constructed. The constituent to the right is right headed and the second constituent is left headed. The heads of both constituents are projected on line 1 along with the degenerate foot. These heads are subsequently projected on line 2 where a binary left headed constituent is constructed whose head is projected on line 3. As expected, a secondary stress occurs on the penultimate syllable.

The next sextasyllabic nominal structure (CVC CV CVC CV CVV' CV) is exemplified in (4.3.3.6.5).

    4.3.3.6.5

```
Ɣet ti noy tu noo ɗo
(*)(*  *)(*  *) <*>       0
(*)   (*   *)            1
(*         *)            2
      *                 3
```

In (4.3.3.6.5) the last syllable is marked extra metrical on line 0 where two binary constituents and one degenerate foot are constructed. The heads of both constituents are projected on line 1 along with the degenerate foot. On line 1 a binary right headed constituent is constructed whose head is projected on line 2 along with the head of the degenerate foot. A binary right headed constituent is then constructed whose head is projected on line 3. Conflating lines 2 and 3 results in the following structure.

```
Yet ti noy tu noo do
(*) (* *) (* *) <*>     0
(*)   (*    *)          1
          *            2
```

As expected, secondary stresses occur on the first syllable and third syllables.

The next sextasyllabic nominal complex structure (CV CV nCV CVC CVV' CV) is exemplified in (4.3.3.6.6).

    4.3.3.6.6

```
na no ndi ran noo be
(*) (*  *)(*   *) <*>    0
(*) (*        *)         1
(*            *)         2
          *            3
```

In (4.3.3.6.6) the last syllable is marked extrametrical on line 0 where two binary constituents and one degenerate foot are constructed. The heads of the constituents and the degenerate foot are projected on line 1 where a binary right headed constituent and a degenerate foot are constructed. The heads are projected on line 2 where a binary right headed constituent is constructed whose head is projected on line 3. Conflating lines 1 and 2 leads to the structure in (4.3.3.6.7)

    4.3.3.6.7

```
na no ndi ran noo be
(*) (*  *) (*  *) <*>    0
(*           *)         1
          *            2
```

The application of the second stress deletion rule eliminates the incorrectly placed secondary stress on the first syllable.

The next sextasyllabic nomimal complex structure (CVV'C CV nCV CVC CVV CV) is exemplified in (4.3.3.6.8).

4.3.3.6.8
tiiɗ no ndi ran noo ɓe
naat no ndi ran noo ɓe
```
(*)  (*   *)(*   *)  <*>   0
(*)  (*        *)          1
(*             *)          2
 *                        3
```

In (4.3.3.6.8) the last syllable is marked extrametrical on line 0 where two binary right headed constituents and one degenerate foot are constructed. The heads are projected on line 1 where a binary right headed constituent and a degenerate foot are constructed. The heads are projected on line 2 where a binary left headed constituent is constructed whose head is projected on line 3. Conflating lines 1 and 2 leads to the structure in (4.3.3.6.9).

4.3.3.6.9
tiiɗ no ndi ran noo ɓe
naat no ndi ran noo ɓe
```
(*)  (*   *)(*   *)  <*>   0
(*             *)          1
 *                        2
```

As predicted, a secondary stress occurs on the penultimate syllable.
The next sextasyllabic nominal complex structure (CVC CVC CVC CV CVV' CV) is exemplified in (4.3.3.6.10).

4.3.3.6.10
jol tin toy tu noo ɗo
```
(*) (*   *) (*   *)  <*>     0
(*) (*          *)          1
(*              *)          2
 *                         3
```

In (4.3.3.6.10), the last syllable is marked extrametrical on line 0 where two binary constituents and one degenerate foot are constructed. The heads are projected on line 1 where a binary right headed constituent and one degenerate foot are constructed. The heads are projected on line 2 where a binary right headed constituent is constructed whose head is projected on line 3. Conflating lines 1 and 2 eliminates the incorrectly placed secondary stress on the second syllable as illustrated in the following structure.

```
jol tin toy tu noo do
(*) (*   *) (*  *) <*>     0
(*) (*       *)          1
(*           *)          2
             *           3
```

The next sextasyllabic nominal complex structure (CVC CV nCV CVC CVV' CV) is exemplified in (4.3.3.6.11).

4.3.3.6.11
```
lom to ndi  roy noo be
(*) (*  *)(*  *) <*>     0
(*) (*       *)          1
(*           *)          2
             *           3
```

In (4.3.3.6.11), the last syllable is marked extrametrical on line 0 where two binary constituents and one degenerate foot are constructed. The heads are projected on line 1 where a binary right headed constituent and one degenerate foot are constructed. The heads are projected on line 2 where a binary right headed constituent is constructed whose head is projected on line 3. Conflating lines 1 and 2 results in the structure in (4.3.3.6.12).

4.3.3.6.1.2
```
lom to ndi  roy noo be
(*) (*  *)(*  *) <*>     0
(*           *)          1
             *           2
```

The next sextasyllabic nominal complex structure (CVC CV CV CV CVV' CV) is exemplified in (4.3.3.6.13).

4.3.3.6.13
```
god di ki  no yii do
(*)  (* *) (* *) <*>     0
(*)  (*      *)          1
(*           *)          2
             *           3
```

In (4.3.3.6.13) the first syllable is marked exrametrical on line 0 where two binary constituents and one degenerate foot are constructed. The heads are projected on line 1 where a binary right headed constituent and one degenerate foot are constructed. The heads are projected on line 2 where a binary right headed constituent is constructed whose head is projected on line 3.

In addition to sextasyllabic complexes, the proposed analysis is tested against septasyllabic complexes to further determine its adequacy.

4.3.3.7 Septasyllabic Complexes

The first septasyllabic nominal complex structure (CVC CV CV CVC CV CVV' CV) is exemplified in (4.3.3.7.1).

    4.3.3.7.1
        joʈ ʈi ti noy tu noo ɗo
        moʈ ʈi ti noy tu noo ɗo
        (*   *)(* *) (* *) <*>   0
        (*)   (*   *)   1
        (*   *)   2
                       *   3

In (4.3.3.7.1) the last syllable is marked extra metrical on line 0 where three binary constituents are constructed. The ones to the right are right headed and the ones to the left are left headed. The heads are projected on line 1 where a binary right headed constituent and a degenerate foot are constructed. The heads are then projected on line 2 where a binary right headed constituent is constructed whose head is projected onto line 3.

The next septasyllabic nominal complex structure (CVC CV nCV CVC CV CVV' CV) is exemplified in (4.3.3.7.2).

    4.3.3.7.2
        lom to ndi roy tu noo ɓe
        wos to ndi roy tu noo ɓe
        (*   *) (* *)(* *) <*> 0
        (*)   (*   *)   1
        (*   ᵐ*)   2
                       *   3

In (4.3.3.7.2) the last syllable is marked extrametrical on line 0 where two binary right headed constituents and a left headed constituent are constructed. The heads are projected on line 1 where a binary right headed constituent and a degenerate foot are constructed. The heads are then projected on line 2 where a binary right headed constituent is constructed whose head is projected on line 3. Conflating lines 2 and 3 results in the structure in (4.3.3.7.3).

4.3.3.7.3
wos to ndi roy tu noo ɓe
(* *)	(* *)	(* *)	<*>	0
(*)		(* *)		1
		*		2

As expected, a secondary stress occurs on the first syllable.
The next septasyllabic nominal complex structure (CVVC CV nCV
CVC CV CVV CV) is exemplified in (4.3.3.7.4).

4.3.3.7.4
tiid̃ no ndi roy tu noo ɓe
(* *)	(* *)	(* *)	<*>	0
(*)		(* *)		1
(*		*)		2
*				3

In (4.3.3.7.4), the last syllable is marked extrametrical on line 0 where
two binary right headed constituents and one left headed constituent are
constructed. The heads are projected on line 1 where a binary right headed
constituent and a degenerate foot are constructed. The heads are projected
on line 2 where a binary left headed constituent is constructed whose head
is projected on line 3. Conflating lines 2 and 3 yields the structure in
(4.3.3.7.5)

4.3.3.7.5
tiid̃ no ndi roy tu noo ɓe
(* *)	(* *)	(* *)	<*>	0
(*)		(* *)		1
*				3

As expected, secondary stresses occurs on the fourth and penultimate
syllables.
The next septasyllabic nominal complex sructure (CVC CV nCVC CV
CVC CVV CV) is exemplified in (4.3.3.7.6)

4.3.3.7.6
hol lo ndir ki nan noo ɓe
(* *)	(* *)	(* *)	<*>	0
(*)	(*	*)		1
(*		*)		2
		*		3

In (4.3.3.7.6) the last syllable is marked extrametrical on line 0 where three binary constituents are constructed. The ones to the left are left headed while the one to the right is right headed. The heads are projected on line 1 where a binary right headed constituent and a degenerate foot are constructed. The heads are projected on line 2 where a binary right headed constituen is constructed whose head is projected on line 3.

The next septasyllabic nominal complex structure (CVV' CV CVC CV CVC CVV CV) is exemplified in (4.3.3.7.7).

    4.3.3.7.7

    loo to tir ki nan noo ɓe

    (*   *)(* *) (*   *) <*> 0

    (*)   (*   *)   1

    (*   *)   2

    *   3

In (4.3.3.7.7) the last syllable is marked extrametrical on line 0 where three binary constituents are constructed. The ones to the left are left headed and the one to the right is right headed. The heads are projected on line 1 where a binary right headed constituent and a degenerate foot are constructed. The heads are projected on line 2 where a binary left headed constituent is constructed whose head is projected on line 3.

The next septasyllabic nominal complex structure (CVV'C CVVC CV nCVC CV CVV CV) is exemplified in (4.3.3.7.8).

    4.3.3.7.8

    naat naat to ndir tu noo ɓe

    (*   *) (* *)(* *) <*>   0

    (*)   (* *)   1

    (*   *)   2

    *   3

In (4.3.3.7.8) the last syllable is marked extrametrical on line 0 where two binary right headed constituents and one degenerate foot are constructed. The heads are projected on line 1 where a binary right headed constituent and one degenerate foot are constructed. The heads are projected on line 2 where a binary left headed constituent is constructed whose head is projected on line 3.

The next septasyllabic nominal complex structure (CVC CVC CV CVC CV CVV' CV) is exemplified in (4.3.3.7.9).

4.3.3.7.9
joˠ ˠin tu noy tu noo ɓe
(*   *) (*   *) (* *) <*> 0
(*)   (*   *)   1
(*   *)   2
             *   3

In (4.3.3.7.9) the last syllable is marked extrametrical on line 0 where three binary constituents are constructed. The ones to the right are right headed while the one to the left is left headed. The heads are projected on line 1 where a binary right headed constituent and one degenerate foot are constructed. The heads are projected on line 2 where a binary right headed constituent is constructed whose head is projected on line 3. Conflating lines 2 and 3 results in the structure in (4.3.3.7.10).

4.3.3.7.10
joˠ ˠin tu noy tu noo ɓe
(*   *) (*   *) (* *) <*> 0
(*)   (*   *)   1
             *   2

As expected, secondary stresses occur on the first and fourth syllables
The next septasyllabic nominal complex structure (CVV'C CVVC CV nCV CVC CVV CV) is exemplified in (4.3.3.7.11).

4.3.3.7.11
naat naat to ndi ran noo ɓe
(*   *) (*   *)(*   *) <*>   0
(*)   (*   *)   1
(*   *)   2
*   3

In (4.3.3.7.11) the last syllable is marked etrametrical on line 0 where three constituents are constructed. The heads are projected on line 1 where a binary right headed constituent and one degenerate foot are constructed. The heads are projected on line 2 where a binary left headed constituent is constructed whose head is projected on line 3.

The next septasyllabic nominal complex structure (CV CV CV CVC CV CVV CV) is exemplified in (4.3.3.7.12).

4.3.3.7.12
ca bo bi noy tu noo ɗo
(* *)(* *) (* *) <*>   0
(*)   (*   *)   1
(*   *)   2
               *   3

In (4.3.3.7.12) the last syllable is marked extrametrical on line 0 where three binary constituents are constructed. The ones to the right are right headed and the one to the left is left headed. The heads are projected on line 1 where a binary right headed and one degenerate foot are constructed. The heads are projected on line 2 where a binary right headed contituent is constructed whose head is projected on line 3. Conflating lines 2 and 3 results in the structure in (4.3.3.7.13).

4.3.3.7.13
ca bo bi noy tu noo ɗo
(* *)(* *) (* *) <*>   0
(*)   (*   *)   1
              *   2

The application of the second stress deletion rule eliminates the incorrectly place secondary stress on the first syllable.

In addition to septasyllabic nominal complexes, the proposed analysis is tested against octasyllabic nominal complexes to further determine its adequacy.

4.3.3.8 Octasyllabic Complexes

The first octasyllabic nominal complex structure (CVC CV nCVC CV CVC CV CVV' CV) is illustrated in (4.3.3.8.1)

4.3.3.8.1
wal lo ndir ti noy tu noo ɓe
hol lo ndir ti noy tu noo ɓe
(*) (* *) (* *) (* *) <*>   0
(*   *) (*   *)   1
(*   *)   2
                  *   3

In (4.3.3.8.1) the last syllable is marked extrametrical on line 0 where three binary right headed constituents and one degenerate foot are constructed. The heads are then projected on line 1 where two binary constituents are constructed. The one to the right is right headed and the one to the left is left headed. The heads are projected on line 2 where a binary right headed constituent is constructed whose head is projected on line 3. Conflating lines 2 and 3 leads to the structure in (4.3.3.8.2).

4.3.3.8.2
hol lo ndir ti noy tu noo ɓe
(*) (*   *) (* *) (* *) <*>   0
(*   *)   (*   *)   1
              *   2

As expected, secondary stresses occur on the first, third and fifth syllables.
The next octasyllabic nominal complex structure (CVV CV nCVC CV CVC CV CVV CV) is exemplified in (4.3.3.8.3).

4.3.3.8.3
ɓaa ro ndir ti noy tu noo ɓe
(*) (*   *) (* *) (* *) <*>   0
(*   *)   (*   *)   1
(*   *)   2
 *   3

In (4.3.3.8.3) the last syllable is marked extrametrical on line 0 where three binary right headed constituents and one degenerate foot are constructed. The heads are projected on line 1 where two binary constituents are constructed. The one to the right is right headed while the one to the left is left headed. The heads are then projected onto line 2 where a binary left headed constituent is constructed whose head is projected on line 3.
The next octasyllabic nominal complex structure (CVC CV nCV CVC CV CVC CVV' CV) is exemplified in (4.3.3.8.4).

4.3.3.8.4
lom to ndi roy ki nan noo ɓe
(*) (*   *)(* *)(*   *) <*>   0
(*   *) (*   *)   1
(*   *)   2
 *   3

In (4.3.3.8.4) the last syllable is marked extrametrical on line 0 where three binary constituents and one degenerate foot are constructed. The heads are projected on line 1 where two binary constituents are constructed whose heads are projected on line 2 where a binary right headed constituent is constructed. The head is projected on line 3.

4.3.3.9 Nominals with Suffixes

The derivational suffixes in question are "-am (possessive suffix), -ji (plural suffix),-el/al"(diminutive and augmentative suffixes respectively).

The behavior of derivational suffixes with respect to stress assignment is very revealing. Some derivational suffixes influence the placement of the major stress while others do not.

The first component of this section deals with the use of derivational suffixes which do not affect the placement of the major stress. The derivational suffix analyzed is "-am", the first person singular possessive marker. Data exemplifying this suffix is illustrated in (4.3.3.9.1).

4.3.3.9.1

```
co'k tir ga lam
ɓo'f tir ga  lam
(*) (*  *)<*>    0
(*    *)          1
 *                2
```

In (4.3.3.9.1), except the last syllable, all syllables have the CVC structure. The major stress falls on the first syllable as expected. On line 0 the last syllable is marked extrametrical. A binary left headed foot and a degenerate foot are constructed. On line 1 a left headed constituent is constructed since the two syllables have equal sonority. The head is then projected on line 2. The stress deletion rule 1 eliminates the secondary stress on line 1 and the correct output is derived in (4.3.3.9.2).

4.3.3.9.2

```
ɓo'f tir ga lam
(*) (*  *)<*>    0
 *                1
 *                2
```

Other nominals used with the possessive suffix "-am" display a similar stress pattern as illustrated in 4.3.3.9.3).

4.3.3.9.3 daa' so lam
           baa' ga lam
           (*   *)<*>   0
            *   1

As observed in four syllable nominal words, the major stress falls on the first syllable of the word if that syllable is of the type CV or CVC. The first syllables in (4.3.3.9.3) are of the CV pattern. The major stress falls on the first syllable of the word as predicted by the analysis.

Another suffix which affects stress assignment is the plural suffix -ji. The addition of this plural suffix to certain singular nouns can create conditions leading to the forward shifting of the major stress as in (4.3.3.9.4).

4.3.3.9.4 ɓa taa' ke
           ka baa' ru
           (* *) <*>   0
            *   1

In (4.3.3.9.4) the major stress falls on the penult, the only heavy syllable in the word. This stress assignment is consistent with the stress assignment principles formulated earlier.

The addition of the plural suffix to the forms in (4.3.3.9.4) changes their structure in two ways. First, the vowel of the singular penultimate syllable is no longer heavy. The vowel of the last syllable of the singular form is lengthened and the primary stress of the word is assigned to it as in (4.3.3.9.5).

4.3.3.9.5 ɓa ta kee' ji
           (*)(* *) <*>   0
           (*   *)   1
            *   2

Applying the analysis, the last syllable is marked extrametrical. On line 1 a degenerate foot and a binary right headed constituent are built. The heads are projected on line 1 where a right headed constituent is built since the syllable in the right is more sonorous than the one in the left.

The head is then projected on line 2. The stress deletion rule 2 deletes the secondary stress on line 1 and the correct output is derived in (4.3.3.9.6).

4.3.3.9.6
ɓa ta kee' ji
(*)(* *) <*>   0
(*   *)   1
*   2

Other types of suffixes that affect stress assignment are the dimimutive and augmentative suffixes. In both their singular and plural forms, the addition of the diminutive or the augmentative suffix affects stress placement. The singular forms of the diminutive and augmentative suffixes are -el and -al respectively.

Unlike the plural suffix -ji which causes the forward shifting of the major stress, the diminutive and augmentative suffixes can lead to the retraction of the major stress. The types of stress patterns associated with this structure are illustrated in (4.3.3.9.7) and (4.3.3.9.8).

4.3.3.9.7   4.3.3.9.8
ɓa taa'ke + el/al ---> ɓa'ta kel/kal
ka baa'ru + el/al ---> ka'ba rel/ral

Comparing (4.3.3.9.7) and (4.3.3.9.8), the stress retracts to the first syllable of the word. As predicted by the analysis, since the last syllable of the word is extrametrical, the major stress falls on the first syllable of the word when there is no heavy syllable in the word other than the last syllable. Prior to the addition of the diminutive/augmentative suffixes, the metrical structure of "ɓataake" is provided in (4.3.3.9.9).

4.3.3.9.9
ɓa taa' ke
(* *) <*>   0
*   1

The addition of the diminutive/augmentative suffixes leads to the restructuring of the previous constituents as in (4.3.3.9.10).

4.3.3.9.10
ɓa' ta kel
(* *)<*>   0
*   1

The long vowel has been shortened and the major stress falls by default on the first syllable of the word. Three different types of suffixes have been analyzed in this section. The first type does not affect or influence the assignment of the major stress. The second type causes the forward shifting of the stress while the third type causes the retraction of the major stress.

Another type of suffix whose behavior is different from the types discussed is analyzed in the section dealing with stress assignment on verbal complexes.

The adopted analysis accounts neatly for all types of stress assignment patterns in two, three, four and five syllable word nominals using sonority hierarchy. The same analysis used for nominal complexes is retained for verbal complexes. Here again, the analysis is applied to all types of verbal complexes that occur in the language.

4.3.4 Verbal complexes

The stress patterns of verbal complexes vary according to the structure of the syllables in the verb.

4.3.4.1 Monosyllabic Verbs

As expected, in monosyllabic verbal complexes, the major stress occurs on the only syllable of the word. Monosyllabic structures are illustrated in (4.3.4.1.1).

    4.3.4.1.1
       ar
       naat
       hel
       (*)   0
       *   1

4.3.4.2 Disyllabic Verbs

The disyllabic verbs analyzed here consist of a root syllable followed by the infinitival suffix "de". The infinitival suffix is extrametrical. Its presence does not influence the assignment of stress in verbal complexes in Pulaar. The assignment of major stress for two syllable words is straight forward. Since the major stress is never assigned to the infinitival suffix, it falls on the other remaining syllable as in (4.3.4.2.1).

4.3.4.2.1)

      a'r de
     ya'h de
    haa'l de
    (*)   <*>   0
     *   1

As predicted by the analysis, the major stress falls on the first syllable of the word.

4.3.4.3 Trisyllabic Verbs

All possible patterns of trisyllabic verbal complexes are analyzed in this section. The first combination, a CVC CV' CV structure, is illustrated in (4.3.4.3.1).

4.3.4.3.1

        da raa' de
        he ɗaa' de
        (* *) <*>   0
          *   1

Another type of trisyllabic verbal complex has the CV CV'C CV structure as in (4.3.4.3.2).

4.3.4.3.2

        he li'r de
        fi ji'r de
        (* *) <*>   0
          *   1

On line 0 a binary right headed foot is constructed since the left syllable in the constituent is less sonorous than the right constituent. The head of this constituent is projected onto line 1 thus indicating the placement of the major stress.

Another type of trisyllabic verbal complex in Pulaar has the CV'C CV CV structure as in (4.3.4.3.3).

4.3.4.3.3

        jo'l nu de
        ju'k nu de
        (*   *)<*>   0
          *   1

Applying the proposed analysis, on line 0 a left headed foot is constructed since the left syllable in the constituent is more sonorous than the right syllable. The head of the constituent is then projected onto line 1.
Another type of trisyllabic verbal complex has the CVV'C CV CV structure as in (4.3.4.3.4).

    4.3.4.3.4
          joo'f nu de
          soo'f nu de
          (*   *)<*>   0
           *   1

Applying the proposed analysis, on line 0 a left headed foot is constructed since the left syllable in the constituent is more sonorous than the right syllable. The head of the constituent is then projected onto line 1.
Another type of trisyllabic verbal complex has the CVC CV' CV structure as in (4.3.4.3.5).

    4.3.4.3.5
          w`el taa' de
          h`af taa' de
          (* *) <*>   0
           *   1

On line 0 the last syllable is marked extrametrical and a right headed constituent is constructed since the right syllable in the constituent is more sonorous than the left syllable. The head is then projected on line 1.
Another type of trisyllabic verbal complex has the CVV'C CV CV structure as in (4.3.4.3.6).

    4.3.4.3.6
          ϒee'w taa de
          kee's taa 'de
          (*   *) <*>   0
           *   1

On line 0 the last syllable is marked extrametrical and a left headed constituent is constructed since the left syllable in the constituent is more sonorous than the right syllable. The head is then projected on line 1.

Another type of trisyllabic verbal complex has the CV' CV CV structure as in (4.3.4.3.7).

4.3.4.3.7

daa' gaa de
joo' ɗaa de
ɓoo' raa de
(*   *) <*>   0
*   1

On line 0 the last syllable is marked extrametrical and a left headed constituent is constructed since both syllables have equal sonority. The head is then projected on line 1.

Another type of trisyllabic verbal complex has the CV'C CVC CV structure as in (4.3.4.3.8).

4.3.4.3.8

ma'w nin de
ja'm min de
(*   *) <*>   0
*   1

On line 0, the last syllable of the string is marked extrametrical and a left headed foot is constructed since both syllables in the constituent have equal sonority. The head is then projected on line 1.

The proposed analysis accounts for the metrical structure of the various types of trisyllabic verbal complexes. Next are examined the metrical structures of tetrasyllabic verbal complexes.

4.3.4.4 Tetrasyllabic Verbs

The first type of tetrasyllabic complexes is exemplified in (4.3.4.4.1).

4.3.4.4.1

a'r ti r`oy de
jo'Ɣ Ɣi n`oy de
(*) (*   *) <*> 0
(*   *)   1
*   2

On line 0 the last syllable of the string is marked extrametrical and a binary right headed foot and a degenerate foot are constructed. On line 1 a left headed constituent is constructed since the syllables in the constituent have equal sonority. The head is then projected on line 2. As expected, a secondary stress appears on the penult.

The second type of tetrasyllabic verbal complex structure (C`VC CV nCVV CV) is illustrated in (4.3.4.4.2).

4.3.4.4.2

    w`el si ndaa' de
    l`am Ɣi ndaa' de
    (*) (* *) <*>   0
    (*   *)   1
       *   2

On line 0 the last syllable is marked extrametrical and a binary right headed constituent and a degenerate foot are constructed. The heads are projected on line 1 where a right headed constituent is constructed. The head is then projected on line 2. A secondary stress occurs on the first syllable of the word as expected. The adequacy of the analysis is assessed against the structure (CVV'C CV C`VV CV) in (4.3.4.4.3).

4.3.4.4.3

    faa'l ki s`aa de
    lee'l ki n`aa de
    ɗaa'n ki n`aa de
    (*) (* *) <*>   0
    (*   *)   1
    *   2

On line 0 the last syllable of the string is marked extrametrical and a binary right headed constituent and a degenerate foot are constructed. The heads are projected on line 1. On line 1, a left headed constituent is constructed since the left syllable in the constituent is more sonorous than the right syllable. The head is then projected on line 2. A secondary stress occurs where expected.

The next tetrasyllabic verbal complex structure (CVC CV CVV' CV) is exemplified in (4.3.4.4.4).

4.3.4.4.4

    hur to yaa de
    (*)(* *) <*>   0
    (*   *)   1
       *   2

In (4.3.4.4.4), the last syllable is marked extrametrical on line 0 where a binary right headed constituent and one degenerate foot are constructed. The heads are projected on line 1 where a binary right headed constituent is constructed whose head is projected on line 2. As expected, a secondary stress occurs on the first syllable.

The next tetrasyllabic verbal complex structure (VC CV nCVC CV) is exemplified in (4.3.4.4.5).

4.3.4.4.5

```
      ab bo ndir  de
      (*) (*    *) <*>   0
      (*         *)      1
           *             2
```

In (4.3.4.4.5), the last syllable is marked extrametrical on line 0 where a binary right headed constituent and a degenerate foot are constructed. The heads are projected on line 1 where a binary right headed constituent is constructed whose head is projected on line 2. As predicted, a secondary stress occurs on the first syllable.

The next tetrasyllabic verbal complex structure (CV CV CVV CV) is exemplified in (4.3.4.4.6).

4.3.4.4.6

```
      le  lo yaa de
      (*)(*  *) <*>    0
      (*        *)      1
              *         2
```

In (4.3.4.4.6), the last syllable is marked extrametrical on line 0 where a binary right headed constituent and one degenerate foot are constructed. The heads are projected on line 1 where a binary right headed constituent is constructed whose head is projected on line 2. The application of the second stress deletion rule eliminates the incorrectly placed secondary stress on the first syllable.

The next tetrasyllabic verbal complex structure (V CV nCVC CV) is exemplified in 4.3.4.4.7).

4.3.4.4.7

```
      a do ndir  de
      (*)(*   *) <*>       0
      (*         *)        1
              *            2
```

In (4.3.4.4.7), the last syllable is marked extrametrical on line 0 where a binary right headed constituent and a degenerate foot are constructed. The heads are projected on line 1 where a binary right headed constituent is constructed whose head is projected on line 2. The application of the second stress deletion rule eliminates the incorrectly placed secondary stress on the first syllable.

The next tetrasyllabic verbal complex structure (V CV CVV' CV) is exemplified in (4.3.4.4.8).

    4.3.4.4.8
    a do yaa de
    (*)(* *) <*> 0
    (*   *)   1
        *   2

In (4.3.4.3.8), the last syllable is marked extrametrical on line 0 where a binary right headed constituent and a degenerate foot are constructed. The heads are projected on line 1 where a binary right headed constituent is constructed whose head is projected on line 2. The application of the second stress deletion rule eliminates the incorrectly placed secondary stress on the first syllable.

The next tetrasyllabic verbal complex structure (CV CV CVC CV) is exemplified in (4.3.4.4.9).

    4.3.4.4.9
    sa bo bin de
    (*)(* *) <*>   0
    (*   *)   1
        *   2

In (4.3.4.4.9), the last syllable is marked extrametrical on line 0 where a binary right headed constituent and one degenerate foot are constructed. The heads are projected on line 1.A binary right headed constituent is constructed. The head is projected on line 2. The application of the second stress deletion rule eliminates the incorrectly placed secondary stress.

The next tetrasyllabic verbal complex structure (CVV'C CVVC CV CV) is exemplified in (4.3.4.4.10).

    4.3.4.4.10
    daal daal nu de
    (*) (*   *)<*> 0
    (*   *)   1
        *   2

In (4.3.4.4.10), the last syllable is marked extrametrical on line 0 where a binary right headed constituent and a degenerate foot are constructed. The heads are projected on line 1 where a binary left headed constituent is constructed whose head is projected on line 2. The application of the first stress deletion rule eliminates the incorrectly placed secondary stress on the second syllable.

The adopted analysis has thus far provided an accurate account of the metrical structure of disyllabic, trisyllabic, tetrasyllabic verbal complexes. The adequacy of this analysis is further tested against pentasyllabic verbal complexes.

4.3.4.5 Pentasyllabic Verbs

The first type of pentasyllabic verbal complex structure (C`VC CV CV CVV' CV) is exemplified in (4.3.4.5.1).

4.3.4.5.1

```
l`es di ki naa ' de
w`os to ndi ree' de
(*    *)(*  *) <*>      0
(*         *)            1
       *                 2
```

On line 0 the last syllable is marked extrametrical and two binary constituents are constructed. The constituent to the right is right headed and the one to the left is left headed. The heads are projected on line 1 where a binary right headed constituent is constructed and the head is projected on line 2. As expected, a secondary stress occurs on the first syllable or the word.

The next pentasyllabic verbal complex structure (CV'C CV CV CVC CV) is illustrated in (4.3.4.5.2).

4.3.4.5.2

```
hes di ti noy de
(*    *)(*  *) <*>      0
(*         *)            1
       *                 2
```

In (4.3.4.5.2) the last syllable is marked extra metrical on line 0 where two binary constituents are constructed. The one to the right is right headed and the one to the left is left headed. The heads of both constituents are projected onto line 1 where a binary left headed constituent is constructed whose head is then projected on line 2. As expected, a secondary stress occur on the second CVC syllable in the word.

The next pentasyllabic verbal complex structure (CVV'C CV CV CVV CV) is illustrated in (4.3.4.5.3).

4.3.4.5.3

```
haaŋ ɗi ki naa de
(*      *) (* *)  <*>     0
(*            *)          1
 *                       2
```

In (4.3.4.5.3) the last syllable is marked extra metrical on line 0 where two binary constituents are constructed. The one to the right is right headed and the one to the left is left headed. Both heads are projected onto line 1 where a binary left headed constituent is constructed whose head is then projected onto line 2.

The next pentasyllabic verbal complex structure (CVV'C CVVC CV nCVC CV) is illustrated in (4.3.4.5.4).

4.3.4.5.4

```
naat naat to ndir de
(*    *) (*    *) <*>     0
(*            *)          1
 *                       2
```

In (4.3.4.5.4) the last syllable is marked extra metrical on line 0 where two binary constituents are constructed. The one to the right is right headed and the one to the left is left headed. Both heads are projected on line 1 where a binary left headed constituent is constructed whose head is then projected on line 2. As expected, a secondary stress occurs on the CVC syllable.

The next pentasyllabic verbal complex structure (CV CV nCVC CVC CV) is exemplified in (4.3.4.5.5).

4.3.4.5.5

```
da ɗo ndi roy de
(*  *) (*  *)  <*>     0
(*          *)         1
 *                    2
```

In (4.3.4.5.5) the last syllable is marked extrametrical on line 0 where two binary constituents are constructed. The heads are projected on line 1 where a binary right headed constituent is constructed whose head is projected on line 2. The application of the second stress deletion rule eliminates the incorrectly placed secondary stress on the first syllable.

The next pentasyllabic verbal complex structure (VC CV CV CVV' CV) is exemplified in (4.3.4.5.6).

4.3.4.5.6

ab bi to yaa de

```
(*  *)( *  *) <*> 0
(*          *)      1
        *         2
```

In (4.3.4.5.6), the last syllable is marked extrametrical on line 0 where two binary constituents are constructed. The heads are projected on line 1 where a binary right headed constituent is constructed whose head is projected on line 2. As expected, a secondary stress occurs on the first syllable.

The next pentasyllabic verbal complex structure (CV CV CV CVC CV) is exemplified in (4.3.4.5.7).

4.3.4.5.7

sa bo bi noy de

```
(*  *)( *  *) <*>  0
(*          *)      1
        *         2
```

In (4.3.4.5.7) the last syllable is marked extrametrical on line 0 where two binary constituents are constructed. The heads are projected on line 1 where a binary right headed constituent is constructed whose head is projected on line 2. The application of the second stress deletion rule eliminates the incorrectly placed secondary stress on the first syllable.

The next pentasyllabic verbal complex structure (CVC CVC CV CVV CV) is exemplified in (4.3.4.5.8).

4.3.4.5.8

nan tin ti noy de

```
(*  *) ( *  *) <*> 0
(*            *)     1
        *          2
```

In (4.3.4.5.8), the last syllable is marked extrametrical on line 0 where two binary constituents are constructed whose heads are projected on line 1 where a binary right headed constituent is constructed whose head is projected on line 2. As expected, a secondary stress occurs on the first syllable of the word.

The next pentasyllabic verbal complex structure (VC CV CV CVV CV) is exemplified in (4.3.4.5.9).

    4.3.4.5.9

       as ki ti naa de
       (* *)(* *) <*>   0
       (*   *)   1
          *   2

In (4.3.4.5.9), the last syllable is marked extrametrical on line 0 where two binary constituents are constructed whose heads are projected on line 1 where a binary right headed constituent is constructed whose head is projected on line 2. As expected, a secondary stress occurs on the first syllable.

In addition to pentasyllabic verbal complex structures, the adequacy of the proposed analysis is tested against various sextasyllabic structures.

4.3.4.6 Sextasyllabic Verbs

The first sextasyllabic verbal complex structure (CVC CV CV CV CVV' CV) is exemplified in (4.3.4.6.1).

    4.3.4.6.1
    jab bi ki no yaa de
    hol li ki no yaa de
    wuj ji ki no yaa de
    (*) (* *)(* *) <*>   0
    (*) (*   *)   1
    (*   *)   2
       *   3

In (4.3.4.6.1) the last syllable is marked extra metrical on line 0 where two binary right headed constituents and a degenerate foot are constructed. The heads of the constituents are then projected on line 1 along with the degenerate foot. On line 1 a binary right headed constituent is constructed whose head is projected on line 2 long with the head of the degenerate foot. On line 2 a binary right headed constituent is constructed whose head is projected on line 3. Conflating lines 1 and 2 results in the following structure.

```
jab bi ki no yaa de
hol li ki no yaa de
wuj ji ki no yaa  de
(*) (* *)(* *) <*>        0
(*              *)        1
                *        2
```

A secondary stress occurs, as expected, on the first syllable.
The next sextasyllabic verbal complex structure (CVV'C CV CV CV CVV CV) is exemplified in (4.3.4.6.2).

4.3.4.6.2
```
haaŋ ɗi ki no yaa  de
(*)  (* *)(* *) <*>        0
(*)  (*         *)        1
(*              *)        2
 *                        3
```

In (4.3.4.6.2), the last syllable is marked extra metrical on line 0 where two binary constituents and one degenerate foot are constructed. The head of both constituents are projected on line 1 along with the degenerate foot. On line 1, a binary right headed constituent is constructed whose head is projected on line 2 along with the head of the degenerate foot. A binary left headed constituent is constructed on line 2 whose head is projected on line 3. Conflating lines 1 and 2 results in the following structure.

```
haaŋ ɗi ki no yaa de
(*) (* *)(* *) <*>        0
(*              *)        1
 *                        2
```

As expected, a secondary stress occurs on the penultimate syllable.
The next sextasyllabic verbal complex structure (CV'C CV CVC CV CVC CV) is exemplified in (4.3.4.6.3).

4.3.4.6.3
```
les ɗi tin ti noy de
(*) (* *) (* *) <*>        0
(*)  (*      *)        1
(*           *)        2
 *                    3
```

In (4.3.4.6.3), the last syllable is marked extrametrical on line 0 where two binary right headed constituents and one degenerate foot are constructed. The heads are projected on line 1 where a binary left headed constituent and one degenerate foot are constructed. The heads are projected on line 2 where a binary left headed constituent is constructed whose head is projected on line 3. Conflating lines 2 and 3 results in the structure in(4.3.4.6.4).

4.3.4.6.4

```
les di tin  ti noy de
(*) (* *) (* *) <*>      0
(*)   (*    *)           1
*                        2
```

The next sextasyllabic verbal complex structure (CVC CVC CV CV CVV' CV) is exemplified in (4.3.4.6.5).

4.3.4.6.5

```
yan kin ti no yaa de
(*) (* *)(* *) <*>       0
(*) (*      *)           1
(*          *)           2
*                        3
```

In (4.3.4.6.5), the last syllable is marked extrametrical on line 0 where two binary constituents and one degenerate foot are constructed. The heads are projected on line 1 where a binary right headed constituent and a degenerate foot are constructed. The heads are projected on line 2 where a binary right headed constituent is constructed whose head is projected on line 3. Conflating lines 1 and 2 results in the structure in (4.3.4.6.6).

4.3.4.6.6

```
yan kin ti no yaa de
(*) (* *)(* *) <*>       0
(*          *)           1
*                        2
```

As expected, a secondary stress occurs on the first syllable.

The next sextasyllabic verbal complex structure (CVV' CV CV CV CVV CV) is exemplified in (4.3.4.6.7).

4.3.4.6.7
    aas ti ki no yaa de
    (*) (* *)(* *) <*>   0
    (*) (*   *)   1
    (*   *)   2
    *   3

In (4.3.4.6.7), the last syllable is marked extrametrical on line 0 where two binary constituents and one degenerate foot are constructed. The heads are projectd on line 1 where a binary right headed constituent and one degenerate foot are constructed. The heads are projected on line 2 where a binary left headed constituent is constructed whose head is projected on line 3. Conflating lines 1 and 2 leads to the structure in (4.3.4.6.8).

    aas ti ki no yaa de
    (*) (* *)(* *) <*>   0
    (*   *)   1
    *   2

As expected, a secondary stress occurs on the penultimate syllable.
The next sextasyllabic verbal complex structure (CVV'C CV CV CVV CV) is exemplified in (4.3.4.6.9).

4.3.4.6.9
    taas ti ki no   yaa de
    seer ni ki no yaa de
    (*) (* *)(* *) <*>   0
    (*) (*   *)   1
    (*   *)   2
    *   3

In (4.3.4.6.9), the last syllable is marked extrametrical on line 0 where two binary constituents and one degenerate foot are constructed. The heads are projected on line 1 where a binary right headed constituent and a degenerate foot are constructed. The heads are projected on line 2 where a binary left headed constituent is constructed whose head is projected on line 3. Conflating lines 1 and 2 leads to the structure in (4.3.4.6.10).

4.3.4.6.10
   aas ti ki no yaa de
   (*) (* *)(* *) <*>   0
   (*   *)   1
   *   2

As expected, a secondary stress occurs on the penultimate syllable. The next sextaysllabic verbal complex structure (VC CV CV CV CVV' CV) is exemplified in (4.3.4.6.11).

4.3.4.6.11
   aw ɣi ki no yaa de
   (*) (* *)(* *) <*>   0
   (*) (*   *)   1
   (*   *)   2
            *   3

In (4.3.4.6.11), the last syllable is marked extrametrical on line 0 where two binary constituents and one degenerate foot are constructed. The heads are projected on line 1 where a binary right headed constituent and one degenerate foot are constructed. The heads are projected on line 2 where a binary right headed constituent is constructed whose head is projected on line 3. Conflating lines 1 and 2 leads to the structure in (4.3.4.6.12).

4.3.4.6.12
   aw ɣi ki no yaa de
   (*) (* *)(* *) <*>   0
   (*   *)   1
         *   2

As expected, a secondary stress occurs on the first syllable.
The next pentasyllabic verbal complex structure (CVV'C CVVC CV CV CVV CV) is exemplified in (4.3.4.6.13).

4.3.4.6.13)
   daal daal di ki naa de
   (*) (* *)(* *) <*>   0
   (*) (*   *)   1
   (*   *)   2
   *   3

In (4.3.4.6.13), the last syllable is marked extrametrical on line 0 where two binary constituents and one degenerate foot are constructed. The heads are projected on line 1 where a binary left headed constituent and one degenerate foot are constructed. The heads are projected on line 2 where a binary left headed constituent is constructed whose head is projected on line 3. Conflating lines 2 and 3 leads to the structure in (4.3.4.6.14).

4.3.4.6.14

daal daal di ki naa de
(*) (*   *)(* *) <*>   0
(*) (*   *)   1
 *   2

The application of the first stress deletion rule eliminates the incorrectly placed secondary stress on the second syllable as in (4.3.4.6.15).

4.3.4.6.15

daal daal di ki naa de
(*) (*   *)(* *) <*>   0
(*)   *   1
 *   2

The next sextasyllabic verbal complex structure (VC CVC CV CV CVV' CV) is exemplified in (4.3.4.6.16).

4.3.4.6.16

as kin ti no yaa de
(*) (* *)(* *) <*>   0
(*) (*   *)   1
(*   *)   2
          *   3

In (4.3.4.6.16), the last syllable is marked extrametrical on line 0 where two binary constituents and one degenerate foot are constructed. The heads are projected on line 1 where one binary constituent and one degenerate foot are constructed. The heads are projected on line 2 where a binary right headed constituent is constructed whose head is projected on line 3. Conflating lines 1 and 2 leads to the structure in (4.3.4.6.17).

4.3.4.6.17

    as kin ti no yaa de

    (*) (* *)(* *) <*>   0

    (*   *)   1

            *   2

As expected, a secondary stress occurs on the first syllable. The next sextasyllabic verbal complex structure (CVVC CVVC CV nCV CVC CV) is exemplified in (4.3.4.6.18).

4.3.4.6.18

    naat naat to ndi roy de

    (*) (*   *) (* *) <*> 0

    (*) (*   *)   1

    (*   *)   2

    *   3

In (4.3.4.6.18), the last syllable is marked extrametrical on line 0 where two binary constituents and one degenerate foot are constructed. The heads are projected on line 1 where a binary left headed constituent and one degenerate foot are constructed. The heads are projected on line 2 where a binary left headed constituent is constructed whose head is projected on line 3. Conflating lines 2 and 3 leads to the structure in (4.3.4.6.19).

4.3.4.6.19

    naat naat to ndi roy de

    (*) (*   *) (* *) <*>   0

    (*) (*   *)   1

    *   2

The application of the first stress deletion rule eliminates the incorrectly placed secondary stress on the second syllable.

The next sextasyllabic verbal complex structure (CVV' CV CVC CV CVV CV) is exemplified in (4.3.4.6.20).

4.3.4.6.20

    loo to tir ki naa de

    (*)(* *)(* *) <*>   0

    (*) (*   *)   1

    (*   *)   2

    *   3

In (4.3.4.6.20), the last syllable is marked extrametrical on line 0 where two binary right headed constituents and one degenerate foot are constructed. The heads are projected on line 1 where a binary right headed constituent and one degenerate foot are constructed. The heads are projected on line 2 where a binary left headed constituent is constructed whose head is projected on line 3. Conflating lines 2 and 3 leads to the structure in (4.3.4.6.21).

4.3.4.6.21
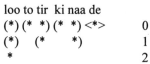

As expected, secondary stresses occur on the third and penultimate syllables.

The next sextasyllabic verbal complex structure (CVC CV CVC CV CVV' CV) is exemplified in (4.3.4.6.22).

4.3.4.6.22
```
Ƴel li toy  ti naa de
(*) (* *) (* *) <*>        0
(*)  (*   *)               1
(*        *)               2
         *                 3
```

In (4.3.4.6.22), the last syllable is marked extrametrical on line 0 where two binary right headed constituents and one degenerate foot are constructed. The heads are projected on line 1 where a binary right headed constituent and one degenerate foot are constructed. The heads are projected on line 2 where a binary right headed constituent is constructed whose head is projected on line 3. Conflating lines 2 and 3 results in the structure in (4.3.4.6. 23).

4.3.4.6.23
```
Ƴel li toy  ti naa de
(*) (* *) (* *) <*>        0
(*)  (*   *)               1
         *                 2
```

As expected, secondary stresses occur on the first and third syllables.

In addition, the adequacy of the proposed analysis is tested against septasyllabic verbal complexes.

4.3.4.7 Septasyllabic verbs

The first septasyllabic verbal complex structure (CVC CV nCVC CV
CV CVV' CV) is exemplified in (4.3.4.7.1).

4.3.4.7.1
lom to ndir ki no yaa de
```
(*    *) (*    *)(*    *) <*>  0
(*)     (*        *)       1
(*              *)         2
 *                        3
```

In (4.3.4.7.1), the last syllable is marked extrametrical on line 0 where
three binary constituents are constructed whose heads are projected on
line 1 where a binary right headed constituent and one degenerate foot are
constructed. The heads are projected on line 2 where a binary right headed
constituent is constructed whose head is projected on line 3. Conflating
lines 2 and 3 leads to the following structure.

lom to ndir ki no yaa de
```
(*    *) (*    *) (*    *) <*>   0
(*)      (*        *)           1
          *                    2
```

The next septasyllabic verbal complex structure (CVC CV CVC CV CV
CVV' CV) is exemplified in (4.3.4.7.2).

4.3.4.7.2
woj ji toy ki no yaa de
```
(*    *)(*    *) (*    *) <*>    0
(*)     (*          *)          1
(*                  *)          2
 *                             3
```

In (4.3.4.7.2), the last syllable is marked extrametrical on line 0 where
three binary constituents are constructed. The heads are projected on line
1 where a binary right headed constituent and a degenerate foot are
constructed. The heads are projected on line 2 where a binary right headed
constituent is constructed whose head is projected on line 3. Conflating
lines 2 and 3 leads to the structure in (4.3.4.7.3).

4.3.4.7.3

woj ji toy ki no yaa de
(*   *)(*   *)(* *) <*> 0
(*)   (*   *)   1
              *   2

As expected, secondary stresses occur on the first and third syllables.

4.3.5 Sentence Metrical Structure

This section focuses on the stress patterns of one, two, three and four word sentences. The analysis of Pulaar sentence metrical structure is somewhat different from word metrical structure. In order to account for sentence metrical structure, the following analysis is proposed

Analysis
-Vowels that are heads of rimes are stress bearing
-The last syllable of the string is not extrametrical
-Line 0 parameters are [+HT, +BND, right to left].
On line 0, construct binary right headed constituents if the left syllable in the constituent is equal to or less sonorous that the right syllable; otherwise construct left headed constituents. Project the head (s) on line 1.
-Line 1 parameter settings are [+HT, BND, right to left].
On line 1, construct binary right headed constituents if the left syllable in the constituent is equal to or less sonorous than the right syllable; otherwise
construct left headed constituents. Project the head(s) on line 2.
-Line 2 parameter settings are [+HT, +BND, right to left]. If necessary, construct right headed constituents on line 2 if the left syllable in the constituent is equal to or less sonorus than the right syllable. Project the head(s) on line 3.

One important difference between this analysis and the one proposed earlier to account for word metrical structure relates to the fact that the last syllable is not extrametrical in the analysis of the metrical structure of sentences. This adaptation is motivated by the fact that adverbials tend to occur in sentence final position. These adverbials generally attract stress as they tend to carry some form of focus as illustrated in the following sentences.

ya'h
ya'hanam
yahanam too'n
yahanam too`n joo'ni

Consequently, it is necessary to adapt this aspect of the analysis. The revised analysis is applied to one, wo, three and four word sentences.

One Word Sentences

The stress patterns of one word sentences are similar to the stress patterns of verbal complexes in isolation. The first type of one word sentence, a one syllable sentence, is illustrated in (4.3.5.1.1).

> 4.3.5.1.1
> ya'h
> a'r
> foo'ɗ
> (*)   0
> *   1

In (4.3.5.1.1), the major stress falls on the only syllable of the word. The next one word sentence type is illustrated in (4.3.5.1.2).

> 4.3.5.1.2
> uddit
> (* *)   0
> *   1

One left headed constituent is constructed on line 0 and the head is projected on line 1.

The next one word sentence type is illustrated in (4.3.5.1.3).

> 4.3.5.1.3
> le loyo
> (*) (* *)   0
> (* *)   1
> *   2

On line 0 a binary left headed constituent and a degenerate foot are constructed. The heads are projected on line 1 where a binary left headed constituent is constructed whose head is projected on line 2. The application of the first stress deletion rule eliminates the incorrectly places secondary stress on the second syllable.

Two Word Sentences

Two word sentences are illustrated by the data in (4.3.2.50).
4.3.2.50
   ar gaa'y
   (*) (*)   0
   (*   *)   1
      *   2

In (4.3.2.50) the major stress falls not on the verb but on the following word. This rule applies to all instances of this type. Applying the analysis to the first instance, degenerate feet are constructed on line 0. The heads of these constituents are projected on line 1 where a right headed constituent is constructed. The head is projected on line 2. As predicted by the analysis, the major stress surfaces at its normal position. The placement of the major stress on the adverb can be attributed to two important considerations one of which relates to vowel length. As it can be observed in (4.3.2.50) the vowels in the adverbs are much longer than those in the verbs. The other factor is that the focus in these types of sentences rests on the adverb. Actually, the second factor is the one responsible for the assignment of the major stress to the adverbs as illustrated in the data in (4.3.2.51).
   4.3.2.51
         haal joo'ni
         (*) (*   *)   0
         (*   *)   1
            *   2

         daano too'n
         suudo gaa'y
         (*   *)(*)   0
         (*   *)   1
            *   2

The verbs in (4.3.2.51) have long vowels. However, the major stress does not fall on the long vowel of these verbs but on the adverb. Applying the analysis, on line 0 a degenerate foot and a left headed constituent are constructed. The heads are then projected on line 1 where a binary right headed constituent is constructed. The head is then projected on line 2.

Three Word Sentences

Three word sentences are illustrated in (4.3.2.52).

4.3.2.52

```
ar gaay joo'ni
(*) (*)  (*  *)        0
(*) (*     *)          1
(*         *)          2
           *           3
```

```
dum tiidʼii  no fee'wi
(*) (*  *) (*)(*    *)    0
(*      *) (*  *)         1
           (*    *)       2
                 *        3
```

In (4.3.2.52), the major stress shifts and falls on the last word of the sentence. On line 0, degenerate feet and binary constituents are constructed. The heads are projected onto line 1 where right headed constituents are constructed. The heads of the constituents are projected onto line 2 where a right headed constituent is constructed whose head is then projected on line 3. Line 2 is then conflated.

Four Word Sentences

Four word sentences are illustrated in (4.3.2.53).

4.3.2.53

```
ar gaay jooni  joo'ni
(*) (*)  (*  *)(*    *)   0
(*  *)   (*       *)      1
   (*             *)      2
                  *       3
```

The major stress is placed on the first long vowel of the last adverb. On line 0, degenerate and binary feet are constructed whose heads are projected onto line 1. On line 1, binary right-headed constituents are constructed and their heads are projected on line 2 where a right headed binary constituent is constructed. The head is then projected onto line 3. Line 2 is then conflated.

Conclusion

This chapter has provided a comprehensive analysis of Pulaar metrical structure. The proposed analysis accounts for the distribution of word stress. The analysis proposed to account for word stress was revised to account for sentence stress patterns in Pulaar. The application and operation of both analyses were shown throughout the study. Various instances were discussed which render observations by Taylor (1953), Arnott (1970), McIntosh (1984), Prunet and Tellier (1984) inadequate. The assignment of word and sentence stress patterns in Pulaar was successfully accounted for using the sonority hierarchy between the syllables involved. Four levels of weight distinction were motivated even though the framework utilized uses only a two-way-weight distinction.

GLOSSARY

A

a you (singular)
aa interjection
aaɓnu v. make someone fortunate (imperative)
aada (o) custom
aadéé (o) human being
aaltaade (v) to pick/choose
aamiin amen
aamtii v. smells bad (tensed verb)
aamtin v. make smell bad (imperative)
aan you (singular)
aastaa v. is dug up (tensed verb)
aastaade (v) to dig up
aawdi (ndi) seeds for sowing
aaɤto [aacco] chew the cud (imperative)
ababo (ko) type of grass
abbere (nde) grain
acci let go (tensed verb)
addo (ngo) gum disease
addude v. to bring
aduna (o) world
ahde [aade] v. to belch
ahdi [aadi] (o) agreement
alaa no
alfaa title
alkulal (ngal) letter of the alphabet
am v. dance
ami v. danced (tensed verb)
ammin make dance (imperative)
amnu v. make dance (imperative)
amnude v. to make dance
amo (ngo) flood
añaan (o) jealous person
ar v. come (imperative)

ardaade v. to lead
arde (v) to come
ardii v. has led; leads (tensed verb)
ari v. came
arii v. has come (tensed verb)
artaade v. to lead
artiróyde (v) to go and bring back
arwan (o) before
asakal (ngal) tithe
asamaan (o) sky
asi dug up (tensed verb)
asir v. dig with (imperative)
aşkin v. tell someone's lineage (tensed verb)
asko (ngo) genealogy
awɤal (ngal) paddle
ayyiiba (o) vice

B

baabalnaajo (o) person from Baabal
baabiraaɗo (o) father
baabiraagélam (ngél) my little father
baagalam (ngal) my bucket for drawing water
baajól (ngol) strip
baaldigélam (ngél) my little night companion
baali (ɗi) sheep
baalotonooɗo (o) person who used to spend the night
baañoowo (o) hunter
baawaaɗo (o) defeated person
bagi (o) fabric
bagiiji (ɗi) fabrics
bajjo one and only
bala (o) type of fish

balabe (ɗe) shoulders
balla (o) male first name
ballinoowo (o) person who spends/makes spend the night
basotooɗo (o) boastful person
baylo (o) blacksmith
bile (ɗe) traps
bille (ɗe) types of birds
billoowo (o) person who fans away
biloowo (o) charlatan; witchcraft
bonande (nde) harm
bonɗo (o) person who is wicked
bónnu v. spoil (imperative)

ɓ
ɓalal (ngal) wall
ɓale (ɗe) walls
ɓalééwu (ngu) type of fish
ɓalli (ɗi) bodies
ɓataake (o) letter
ɓatakal (ngal) big letter
ɓatakééji (ɗi) letters
ɓatakél (ngél) little letter
ɓóftirgalam (ngal) my tool for picking
ɓoodde (nde) handful of
ɓooraade (v) to remove one's clothing
ɓuri more ... than; better ... than

C
cabbi (ɗi) sticks
caɗi expensive (tensed verb)
caɗti [catti] really expensive
cakalo friendly
cakka (ka) necklace
cakkaaji (ɗi) necklaces

cakkagól (ngól) charity
came (ɗe) disease
cammeeje (ɗe) ends of; ears (i.e. millet ears)
cawal (ngal) big stick
cawél (ngél) little stick
cawon (kon) little sticks
cekke (ɗe) woven fences
celal (ngal) type of grass
céli v. branched (tensed verb)
cellal (ngal) health
célli v. are well (tensed verb)
ciluki (ki) type of tree
cofal (ngal) big baby cheak
cófél (ngél) little baby cheak
cofon (kon) little baby cheaks
cóki v. locked (tensed verb)
cókki (ɗi) chicks
cókki v. pound (tensed verb)
cóktirgalam (ngal) my key
cólgól(ngól) removal of i.e. teeth
cómcól (ngól) a piece of clothing
cóppi (ɗi) baby cheaks

D
daagaade (v) to walk slowly
daasólam (ngól) my trace
daaɣde[daajje] v. to prevent from sucking
dadorde (nde) waist
dahaa (o) ink
damɗi (ɗi) male goats
dara nothing
daraade (v) to stand
daroʃtand/will stand (imperative)
dawaar (o) duuty
debbo (o) woman
débbuus (o) stick
déédi (ɗi) bellies

deeɣ be quiet (imperative)
deeɣɗo [deeɣɣo] (o) a calm person
dééɣnu [dééññu] make quiet (i.e. water) (imperative)
déwél (ngél) little woman
déyum little woman
déɣɣin make quiet (imperative)
dimngal (ngal) animal load
dogde v. to run
dogɗo (o) person who run
dógnu make run (imperative)
dono (o) heir; heiress
dóórumaaru (ndu) large excavation
dów on (top of)
dujal (ngal) island
duwanaaɗo (o) blessed person
duwananooɗo (o) person who was blessed

ɗ
ɗaankinaade (v) to pretend to sleep
ɗaano sleep (imperative)
ɗaanotonooɗo (o) person who used to sleep
ɗojjo (ngo) cough
ɗójju cough (imperative)
ɗum that

E
e and
eeɓ slice (imperative)
ééɓól (ngól) crack; opening
ela disdains (tensed verb)
ella (o) shortcoming
éllééy like; as if
elo iguana

en we (plural)

F
faalkisaade (v) to trivialize
faɗɗu be more elegant (imperative)
fééwi is good (tensed verb)
ferlaade (v) to squat
féɣɣude v. to chop down
fii hit (tensed verb)
fijde [fijje] v. to play
fijirde (nde) game
fijirde (v) to play with
fittude v. to sweep
fodoore (nde) God's wish
fotde [fodde] (nde) duty
fotde [fodde] v. to fit
fówru (ndu) hyenna

G
gaastirgélam (ngél) my little tool for digging
gaastotooɗo (o) person who digs up
gaay here
gabbe (ɗe) grains
gadano first
galle (o) compound
gallééji (ɗi) compounds
gasɗe (ɗe) holes; excavations
gaynaako (o) herdsman
gerte (ɗe) peanuts
gese (ɗe) farms
gite (ɗe) eyes
giyal (ngal) thorn
giye (ɗe) thorns
gollal (ngal) work
golle (ɗe) works
golloowo (o) worker

gollorde (nde) work place
goo one
gorko male
gude (ɗe) sarongs
gujjo (o) thief
gumɗo (o) blind person

H
haa until
haacde [haajje] to scream
haal speak (imperative)
haalaa is said (tensed verb)
haalan tell someone; speak for (tensed verb)
haalde (v) to speak
haalnude v. to make speak
haalpulaarʔen (ɓe) speakers of Pulaar
haaranduru (ndu) plentiness i.e. of food
haarde v. to be full
haawnii is surprising (tensed verb)
haɓɓu tie (imperative)
haɗde [hadde] v. to prevent
haftaade (v) to rise up
hakke (o) right
halal (kal) possessions
halkaade (v) to perish
halkude (v) to kill
hamdaat (o) weight unit
hamde v. to squeeze
hammaayaróyél kingfisher
happu (o) limit; boundary
harde v. to snore
hasnu ready the dead for burial (imperative)
hasnude v. to make ready for burial
heɓde v. to receive; to reach

héɓtii v. has taken away (tensed verb)
heɗaade (v) to listen
héédnude [héénnude] v. to place in a particular location
heewgno full
helaa is broken (tensed verb)
helde v. to break
héli v. broke (tensed verb)
hélirde (v) to break with
hello (ngo) slap
héltii has broken again (tensed verb)
hesde v. to trim; to cut
hettere (nde) piece of (i.e. meat/land)
heʏde [hejje] to fit
hiirde v. to be late (night)
hijde [hijje] v. to roar
hirde v. to be jealous
hóccu pick up (imperative)
hoɗde [hodde] v. to inhabit
hófru (ndu) knee
hol who (question word)
hóllu v. show (imperative)
hóltii v. has enough clothing (tensed verb)
honde v. to pillage
horde v. to be depleted
hórééru (ndu) relative
huɗo (ko) grass
hulnu v. freighten someone (imperative)
humtude v. to untie
hurtóyaade (v) to move to the husband's compound

I
idaa race

iirtu stir (imperative)
ilam (ɗam) flood
iwdi (ndi) origin

J

jaafotooɗo (o) person who forgives
jaal present condolences (imperative)
jaasuusʔen (ɓe) spies
jaataarnaajo (o) person from Jaataar
jaawngal (ngal) guinea fowl
jal laugh (imperative)
jale (ɗe) hoes
jali laughed (tensed verb)
jalo (ngo) hoe
jaltoowo (o) person who is going out
jamaanu (o) world
jamɗe (ɗe) irons
jamiroowo (o) person who gives permission
jamminde (v) to give directions
jawwu catch fire (imperative)
jeese (ɗe) fronts; faces
jiyaaɗo (o) slave
jóɗɗin put down (imperative)
jogotonooɗo (o) person who used to hold/have
jogotooɗo (o) person who holds
jolɗo person who boarded
jólnude (v) to put in
jóltinoowo (o) person who takes or puts out
jooɗaade (v) to sit down
jooɗɗo pretty
jooɗorde (nde) seat
jóófnude (v) to finish/complete

jookɗo person who cornered
jóóni now
joowre (nde) pile of...
jóʏʏin put down (imperative)
jóʏʏinoowo (o) person who puts something somewhere
jóʏʏinóyde (v) to go and place somewhere
juknude (v) to pawn

K

kaafahi sword
kaaldigélam (ngél) my little interlocutor
kaasamaasnaajo (o) person from Casamance
kaaw (o) uncle
kabaral (ngal) big piece of news
kabarél(ngél) little piece of news
kaɓɓanteeɗo (o) bride
kaŋŋe (o) gold
kelle (ɗe) slaps
ko focus particle
kolangal (ngal) farm land
kolndam (ɗam) lack of clothing
kóppi (ɗi) knees
kórééji (ɗi) relatives
kumba female first name

L

laaɓde v. to be clean
laaɗɗo [laaɗɗo] person who crawled
laamo rule (imperative)
ladde (nde) bush
lamba (o) wrestling arena
lambaaji (ɗi) wrestling arenas
lammin appoint a chief (imperative)

lamndaade v. to ask
lamƔindaade (v) to taste
layyo sacrifice (imperative)
lébbi (ɗi) moons
leefɗo non energetic person
léélii is late
léélkinaade (v) to slow the pace
leem pile wood (imperative)
lehde [leede] v. to breath heavily
lella (ba) antilope
lélli (ɗi) antilopes
lémmin v. make pile wood (imperative)
lésdi (ndi) ground
lésɗikinaade (v) to be humble
letto squint-eyed
lewal (ngal) big flame
lewɓe (ɓe) women
léwél (ngél) little flame
lewlewal (ngal) big flame; big moonlight
léwléwél (ngél) little flame
léwru (ndu) moon
léydi (ndi) country, soil
lóhnu [lóónu] v. wear someone out (imperative)
lomtaade v. to replace
lorso (ko) wheat
lowe (ɗe) shares; pieces
lowre (nde) share; piece

M

maa your (singular referent)
maajɗo [maaƔƔo] person who saluted
maajnu [maaññu] make salute (tensed verb)
maakaa (o) plot
maamaawi (ki) big tree
maantórgélam (ngél) my little mark
maayde v. to die
mahde [maade] v. to build
mahɗo[maaɗo] person who built
mahnu [maanu] make someone build (imperative)
mahtii [maatii] has rebuilt (tensed verb)
maje (ɗe) lightnings
majjere (nde) ignorance; loss
malaaɗo (o) blessed person
malal (o) male first name
malli (ɗi) indirect talks
mallól (ngól) indirect talk
malu (ngu) fortune
marɓugól (ngól) closing on
mata (o) weight measure
mataaji (ɗi) weight measures
mawnikinaare (nde) acting important
mawninde (v) to make big
mawniraaɗo (o) older sibling
mawniraagélam (ngél) my older little or dear sibling
meɗen I am
mehde [meede] v. to stutter
memɗo person who touched
mi I
miijiiɗo (o) person who thought
min we
mo him; her; who
mojde [mojje] v. to cover
mola (ba) baby animal
móli (ɗi) baby animals
mool (o) musical instrument
moolde v. to protect someone
moorde v. to braid
mooƔde[moojje] v. to be eaten by

white ants

morndolde (nde) rolled grain

moⲟ̃ⲟ̃o good

móⲟ̃ⲟ̃u be good (imperative)

mutnu [munnu] v. make sink (imperative)

Muusaa (o) Moses

mb

mbaalu (ngu) sheep

mbandu (o) water holder

mbanduuji (ɗi) waterholders

mbóddi (ndi) snake

N

naanaalde (nde) salted area

naange (nge) sun

naangééji (ɗi) suns

naat enter (imperative)

naatɗo [naaɗɗo] person who entered

naatnu [nɔɔnnu] make enter (imperative)

naattin make enter again (imperative)

nadorde (nde) waist

nagge (nge) cow

najnajilo (o) mysterious person

nanii heard (tensed verb)

nate (ɗe) photographs

nawɗo person who took away

nawi took away (tensed verb)

ne when

newe (ɗe) palms

newre (nde) palm

nóddu call (imperative)

nofal (ngal) big ear

nófél (ngél) little ear

nofon (kon) little ears

nófru (ndu) ear

noogaas (o) twenty

nóppi (ɗi) ears

nuskugól (ngól) triviality

nuwaasoornaajo (o) person from Nouakchott

ND

ndaala (ba) wrestling dress

ndaalaaji (ɗi) wrestling dresses

ndamndi (ndi) male goat

nde when

ndii this

ndiyam (ɗam) water

ndonu (ngu) inheritance

NG

ngalu (ngu) wealth

ngaska (ka) hole; excavation

ngelooba (ba) camel

ngesa (ba) farm

ngilngu (ngu) worm

NJ

njaawa (ba) type of viper

njaayéémnaajo (o) person from njaayéém

njahii went

njalat mi I am laughing

njalay mi I am laughing

njamala (ba) giraffe

njamalaaji (ɗi) giraffes

njamndi (ndi) iron

njaram (ɗam) drink

njeenaari (ndi) gift

njelaari (ndi) charity

njii saw (tensed verb)

njiilaw (o) search

njulli (o) circumcised person

ŋ

ŋurtuŋurtu (o) incessant small
fights

Ñ

ñaam eat (imperative)
ñalawma (o) day
ñalawmaaji (ɗi) days
ñammin v. make eat (imperative)
ñaw (ngu) sickness
ñirɓinaade v. to show an angry
face

O

o she; he
on you (singular); you (plural)
oo this
oon he; she
óórgól (ngól) cow movement to
grazing areas
oto (o) car
óttude v. to groan

P

paɗal (ngal) a big shoe
paɗɗal (ngal) elegance
style
palal (ngal) gate closing pool
pale (ɗe) gate closing pieces of
wood; lower grounds
pelal (ngal) footprint
pellal (ngal) big age group
piilagól (ngól) tying of a scarf
piyananooɗo (o) person who
received contributions
póbbi (ɗi) hyennas
póóftórgélam (ngél) my little
resting place
poolaaɗo (o) defeated person

potat mi I equal/amount to
potay mi I equal/amount to
puccu (ngu) horse
pulaar (o) Pulaar dialect

Q

qirraade v. to ascertain

R

rawaandu (ndu) dog
réédu (ndu) belly
remde v. to hoe
rewɓe (ɓe) women
rókku v. give (imperative)
rókkude v. to give
ruggu v. pound (imperative)

S

saafde v. to milk
saakde v. to scatter
saam v. fall (imperative)
saɗi is expensive (tensed verb)
safde v. to be tasty
sahaa (o) moment
sahde [saade] v. to fry
sakkaade v. to give charity
sammin make fall (imperative)
sawru (ndu) stick
sayyo swing (imperative)
seelde v. to slice
sefde v. to draw up
sehde [seede] v. to carve
sekko (ngo) woven fence
sel deviate (imperative)
selde v. to deviate; to branch
séli branched (tensed verb)
sélli is well (tensed verb)
sélnu make deviate (imperative)
sewde v. to be slim

séwnude v. to make slim
sófru (ndu) baby chick
sokde v. to lock
sóki v. locked (tensed verb)
sókki v. pound (tensed verb)
sóññu v. move slightly (imperative)
sóódnu [sóónnu] make someone buy (imperative)
sóódti [sóótti] bought again (tensed verb)
sóófnu v. make wet; soak (imperative)
sóófnude (v) to wet
sóóftii v. has become tasteless (tensed verb)
soorde v. to put rice in the cooking pot
sorde v. to creep underneath
sowde v. to fold
surde v. to hedge
suuɗo hide (imperative)
suurde v. to cover up a misfortune
suutnu [suunnu] make someone lift (imperative)
suweeraatnaajo (o) person from Zouerate

T

taaniiko (o) his/her grandparent
taaniraaɗo (o) grandparent
tabi found (tensed verb)
tagde v. to create
takkórdi (ndi) glue
talkuru (ndu) charm
tallorde (nde) place for rolling
tata (ka) wall
tataaji (ɗi) walls
taw find (imperative)

tawii found (tensed verb)
taɤɗo [taɤɤo] person who is worn out/dead
tébbuuli (ɗi) meats
teyɗo person who performed a deliberate act
tiiɗii is expensive (tensed verb)
tiinde (nde) forefront
tiine (nde) forefronts
timmu be complete (imperative)
tirɗo person who attached
toon there

U

ubbu bury (imperative)
uddugól (ngól) the closing of
udumere (nde) gate
ummo get up (imperative)
ustagól (ngól) reduction
ustugól (ngól) reduction
uum groan (imperative)

W

waal spend the night (imperative)
waalde v. to spend the night
waatde [waadde] v. to swear
waawnu v. make do something
waaɤde [waajje] v. to sweat
waɗir do with (imperative)
waɗti [watti] has done again (tensed verb)
walabo (ngo) shoulder
wallin make spend the night (imperative)
waraa was killed (tensed verb)
wari killed (tensed verb)
welde v. to be tasty
wélsindaade (v) to be careless
weltaade (v) to be happy

wisde v. to water

wóɗɗóndirde v. to be far apart

woocde [woojje] to pick leaves

wóódnu [wóónnu] make exist (imperative)

wóstóndireede (v) to exchange with another person

woyde v. to weep

wóynu v. make cry

wuddu (ndu) navel

wudere (nde) sarong

wuji robbed (tensed verb)

wujju steal (imperative)

wultii v. withdrew a statement (tensed verb)

wumtude v. to recover one's eyesight

wuro (ngo) town; village

wuyɓe (ɓe) thieves

Y

yaajnu [yaaññu] make wide (imperative)

yaakaare (nde) hope

yah go (imperative)

yahanam go for me (imperative)

yahde [yaade] v. to go

yahi left (tensed verb)

yahii went

yarnu make drink (imperative)

yartii v. has drunk again (tensed verb)

yeeso (ngo) front; face

yertere (nde) peanut

yéttu thank (imperative)

yii saw (tensed verb)

yimnu make sing (imperative)

yo exclamation particle

yonde v. to be enough

yooɗde [yoodde] v. to be pretty

yul pierce (imperative)

ϒ

ϒakkude v. to chew

ϒeewtaade v. to check; to look back

ϒéttéé pick up (imperative)

ϒéttu lift; pick up (imperative)

ϒettude v. to pick

ϒoϒɗo [ϒoϒϒo] person who is smart

REFERENCES

Arnott, D. W. 1970. The Nominal and Verbal Systems of Fula. Oxford: Clarendon Press.

Bakovic, J. Eric. 1995. Geminate Shortening in Fula. Trends in African Linguistics, Volume 1.

Clements, G. N. & Keyser S. J. 1983. CV Phonology: A Generative Theory of the Syllable. Linguistic Inquiry Monograph 9, Cambridge, MA: MIT Press.

Davis, S. 1985a. Syllable Weight in Some Australian Languages. BLS II

-------, S. 1988. Syllable Onsets as a Factor in Stress Rules, Phonology Yearbook, Volume 5, No 1.

Delafosse, Maurice. 1914. Esquisse Generale des Langues de l'Afrique. Paris

Goldsmith, John A.: 1990. Auto Segmental and Metrical Phonology. Basil Blackwell

Greenberg, H. Joseph. 1966. The Languages of Africa. Indiana University, Bloomington.

Halle, M., & J. R. Vergnaud 1987b. An Essay on Stress. Cambridge, Massachusetts: MIT Press.

Hanson, Kristin and Paul Kiparsky. 1996. A Parametric Theory of Poetic Meter. Language, Volume 72, No 2.

Hayes, B. 1989. Compensatory Lengthening in Moraic Phonology, Linguistic Inquiry, Volume 17, No 3.

-------, B. 1995. Metrical Stress Theory: Principles and Case Studies. Chicago: University of Chicago Press.

Hestermann, Ferdinand. 1912. Der Anlautwechsel in der Serersprache in Senegambia, West Africa" in Zeitschrift fur dir Kunde des Morgenlandes, Wien, XXXVI.

Kahn, D. 1976. Syllable-Based Generalization in English Phonology, Ph. D. Dissertaion, MIT, Cambridge.

Kayes, J. J. Lowenstamm, & J. R. Vergnaud 1985. The Internal Structure of Phonological Elements: A Theory of Charm and Government, Phonology Yearbook 2.

Klingenheben, August Von. 1925. Die Permutationen des Biafada und des Ful. ZFES 15.3.

Labouret, H. 1952. La Langue des Peuls ou Foulɓe. IFAN, Dakar.

Levin, J. 1985. A Metrical Theory of Syllabicity. Doctoral Dissertation, MIT, Cambridge, Massachusetts.

Liberman, M. & Prince, A. 1977. On Stress and Linguistic Rhythm. Linguistic Inquiry, Volume 8.

McIntosh, Mary 1984. Fulfulde Syntax and Verbal Morphology. St Edmundsbury Press Ltd.

Meinhof, C. 1912. Die Sprachen der Hamiten. Hamburg.

Paradis, C. 1992. Lexical Phonology and Morphology: The Nominal Classes in Fula. New York: Garland.

--------, C & Jean Francois Prunet 1989. On Coronal Transparency, Phonology Volume 6.

Prince, A. 1983. Relating to the Grid, Linguistic Inquiry, Volume 11.

--------, A and Paul Smolensky. 1993. Optimality Theory: Constraint Interaction in Generative Grammar. Ms., Rutgers University and University of Colorado

Sylla, Yero. 1982. Grammaire Moderne du Pulaar. Dakar, Les Nouvelles Editions Africaines.

Taylor, F. W. 1921. A First Grammar of the Adamawa Dialect of the Fulani Language (Fulfulde). Oxford University Press.

Westermann, D. 1911. Die Sudan Sprachen: Eine Sprachvergleichende Studie. Abhandlugen des Hamburgischen Kolonial Institus.

---------------, D. 1927. Die Westlichen Sudansprachen und Ihre Bexiehungen Zum Bantu. Berlin.

INDEX